Meal Ideas

DASH Diet and Anti Inflammatory Meals for Weight Loss

Tammy Gonzales and Deborah Howard

Copyright © 2013 Tammy Gonzales and Deborah Howard
All rights reserved.

Table of Contents

INTRODUCTION 1

SECTION 1: ANTI INFLAMMATORY DIET 7
    Inflammation Problems 7

THE ANTI INFLAMMATION DIET 9

TIPS FOR COOKING AND EATING RIGHT WHEN ON THE ANTI INFLAMMATORY DIET 13

ARE YOU COOKING RIGHT? 17

DELICIOUS ANTI INFLAMMATORY RECIPES 20
    Baked Teriyaki Chicken 20
    Polynesian Chicken 23
    Turkey Tenderloins 25
    Turkey Curry 27
    Noodle-Free Turkey Lasagna 30
    Black Bean Huevos Rancheros 33
    Quinoa Breakfast Cereal 35
    Hearty Bean Dinner 37
    Quinoa and Black Beans 40
    Meaty Beans and Rice 43
    Lentil Soup 46
    Chicken and Lentils 49
    Curried Lentils 52
    Maple-Flavored Salmon 55
    Grilled Salmon 57
    Baked Garlic Salmon 60
    Salmon Ceviche 62
    Mixed Veggie Salad 64
    Grilled Chicken Cranberry Spinach Salad 66
    Delicious Cucumber Salad 68

    Tofu Salad 70
    Tofu Scramble 72
    Baked Tofu 75
    Lime and Cilantro Tofu 77
    Tofu Watercress Salad 79
    Fruit Salad 81
    Healthy Oatmeal 83
    Banana Nut Breakfast Cereal 85

SECTION 2: DASH DIET 88

WHAT IS THE DASH DIET? 89

What Is Hypertension and Why Is It Dangerous? 90

How Does the DASH Diet Work? 91

DASH STUDY DAILY NUTRIENT GOALS 93

DASH DIET GUIDELINES 94

Using DASH for Weight Loss 95

Intuitive Eating with the DASH Diet 95

Making DASH Dieting Easy 96

EXERCISE AND THE DASH DIET 98

RECIPES FOR THE DASH DIET 99

Appetizers 100
    DASH Spinach Dip 100
    Stuffed Portabella Mushrooms 102
    Crispy Coconut Chicken Fingers 104
    Vegetable Sushi 106
    Fresh Mushroom Quesadillas 108

Beverages 110
    Peanut Butter and Banana Smoothie 110
    No-Booze Margarita 111
    Sugar-free Agua Fresca 112
    Spicy, Sweet and Tangy Herbal Tea 114
    Non-Alcoholic Hurricane Punch 115

Breakfast 116
    Chewy Fruit Bars 116
    Broiled Almond-Banana Toast 118
    DASH-friendly Oatmeal 119
    Healthy Homemade Granola 120
    Toasted Breakfast Sandwich 122

Main Dishes 124
    Simple Grilled Chicken 124
    Basic Barbeque "Pork" Chops 125
    Miso-Marinated Cod 127
    Blackened Beef 129
    Feta-ricotta Greek Pizza 131
    Chinese Restaurant Ginger Beef 133
    Vegetable Medley Pasta Sauce 135
    Portabella Mushroom "Burgers" 137

Sides 139
    Baked Macaroni and Cheese 139
    Spicy Steamed Eggplant with Peanut Sauce 141
    Braised Spring Vegetables 143
    Rice Pilaf with Saffron 145
    Spicy Garlic Green Beans 147

Salads 149
    Spicy Tuna Salad 149
    Tabbouleh with Tomatoes 150
    Edamame Salad 152
    Raw Okra Salad 154
    Tomato-Zucchini Salad with Eggs 156
    Low Cholesterol Potato Salad 158

Soups 160
    Nutrient-packed Kale Soup 160

Meatless Lentil Chili 163
Tangy Carrot Curry 165
Cream of Wild Rice Soup with Fennel 167
Hearty Turkey Soup 169

DASH DIET 5-DAY SAMPLE MENU 171

Modifying the 5-Day Meal Plan 174

CONCLUSION 175

Introduction

This book contains meal plan ideas for those suffering with inflammation and hypertension. Even though the featured diets in this book are the Anti Inflammatory Diet and the DASH Diet anyone who wishes to become healthier and eat right can find many recipes within this book to plan menus for weeks in advance. You can follow one or the other diet or combine the two choosing from each diet plan. The choice is yours.

Let's discuss the two different diet plans starting with the anti-inflammatory diet. Inflammation is what happens when that part of the body is irritated. This can occur on any part or area of the body, such as the joints (arthritis), in the heart (cardiovascular disease), within the arteries (caused from high cholesterol and causes blocked arteries), on the muscles, in the organs, etc. In other words, all areas of the body can be affected by inflammation. The good news is that dieting can help to reduce inflammation and help to treat and sometimes cure the conditions the inflammation causes.

Certain foods help to reduce the inflammation and these foods are featured in the anti inflammation diet section. Healthy fats are very beneficial in fighting inflammation. Using oils high in omega 3 fatty acids are great such as canola oil, flax seed oil, olive oil, and in foods like seeds, nuts, and avocados.

Fruits and vegetables contain anti-oxidants and other minerals, which naturally reduce inflammation. It is best to eat these as fresh and whole when possible for the most benefit. People who suffer from the effects of inflammation they should eat at least five servings of fruits and vegetables a day.

Even foods high in protein will help to reduce inflammation. Eating plenty of fish and seafood will give the body the vitamins and in particular the omega 3 fatty acids that will help to reduce the inflammation. If there are no soy allergies, soy foods help to reduce the inflammation, so eating tofu and tempeh are good. Plant based protein from legumes and peas are good as well as tree nuts.

Cook with olive oil when possible or canola oil which contains the omega 3 fatty acids. Replace red meats with fish and seafood and instead of snacking on junk foods snack on nuts and fruits. Eat brightly colored fruit and vegetables.

When aiming for helping the body to treat inflammation certain foods should be avoided, as they may help to aggravate inflammation. These same foods are classified as junk food so it is beneficial for all people to avoid. These foods include processed foods or "convenient" foods, anything high in sugar and or white flour. Avoid foods like sodas, sugary desserts, saturated fats and trans fats. Nightshade foods are also responsible for aggravating inflammation such as tomatoes and eggplants. Some people report their inflammation issues go away if they simply avoid these foods.

The DASH diet is a diet that helps people with hypertension to better control their blood pressure. When a person is diagnosed with hypertension (high blood pressure), the first line of action is often to change the diet. The DASH diet contains foods that are naturally low in sodium and fat and helps people to better control their blood pressure.

Having hypertension is risky to the health. High blood pressure affects the heart and other areas of the body if not treated, managed and controlled. If high blood pressure is left unchecked and untreated it can damage the heart beyond control. It can cause issues with other organs too and the arteries and veins. The good news is that blood pressure is often very treatable through diet.

If the arteries are affected it can lead to fatal conditions. Ideally, the arteries need to be clear in order to pump blood throughout the body. If high blood pressure is not treated the arteries may develop arteriosclerosis (which means "hard" arteries). The arteries are no longer flexible and the risks of blockages increase. This can lead to heart attacks and strokes, which can be deadly.

The risk for an aneurysm increases if the arteries of the brain become narrow or hard. This happens when the blood cannot pass through the artery and it causes it to balloon out. The artery may then cause a blood clot or may break. Both instances are very grave and survival is very rare when this occurs. This can happen as a result of untreated high blood pressure.

High blood pressures can cause the same thing to happen in the heart and this is called coronary artery disease. If this is not caught and treated a result is a heart attack. If blood pressure remains unchecked, the heart can enlarge because the left side has to work harder to pump the blood through the body. It causes a thickening of the left ventricular.

Kidney damage is another issue caused by high blood pressure; the kidneys can go into failure due to the arteries that lead to them not working right. If high blood pressure is diagnosed the kidneys are normally checked as well for this damage. But the good news is that dieting can help to prevent these horrible health conditions.

With both inflammation and hypertension, weight issues can aggravate the situation. This is why both the anti inflammation diet and the DASH diet are good diets to help with weight loss. Excessive weight puts pressure on the entire body, causing the heart to work harder, and putting pressure on areas that inflammation may aggravate. By losing the weight the conditions either may go away or be managed.

Be sure to drink plenty of water every day, regardless of the reason you need to be on these diets. Water helps to work with the foods to help heal the body. Water is essential every day whether you are "dieting" or not. By drinking the water, you help to cleanse out the impurities and keep the body hydrated. Always seek advice from your health care provider before going on any new diet plan.

Section 1: Anti Inflammatory Diet

An anti-inflammatory diet is highly recommended for those that have health problems, as food can cause inflammation that will make the problems worsen. The truth is that chronic inflammation is actually the cause of a number of diseases, such as cancer, Alzheimer's, and heart disorders. Avoiding foods that cause inflammation is important, but the many natural anti inflammatory foods that you can find in this book will help you to eat healthy and avoid inflammation. You'll find that you can protect your body easily, all by eating the right foods!

Inflammation Problems

You notice swelling when it's on the outside of your body, such as when you injure yourself or you strain your muscles. You'll see the swelling, and it will cause you pain. You'll usually take steps to deal with that swelling, such as by applying ice or using heat to treat the problem.

When it's on the inside, it will take a lot more for you to notice the swelling problems. You won't usually feel the inflammation unless it is very bad, and by then there's usually something seriously wrong. You'll have no idea if there isn't serious inflammation, at least not until your problem has gotten out of control. Whether it's swelling caused by arthritis, cancer, or heart disorders, you want to avoid that inflammation as much as possible.

The Anti Inflammation Diet

The anti inflammation diet isn't a weight loss diet, but it's one that is designed to help you keep your inflammation under control. The anti inflammatory diet menu is filled with top anti inflammatory foods that will help to prevent swelling. Some of the best anti inflammatory foods include:

- **Fish --** Most fish contains Omega-3 fatty acids, which are excellent at fighting swelling. You'll find that salmon is one of the best foods to eat if you want to prevent swelling, making it top on the list of anti inflammatory foods.

- **Olive Oil --** Extra virgin olive oil should be included in all anti inflammatory diets, as the healthy unsaturated fats in the oil will help to fight off infection at its source. It will also protect your heart, so it's a healthy choice for anyone!

- **Kelp --** Kelp and other forms of seaweed are loaded with fiber, but it will also help to fight off swelling. It's rich in antioxidants, meaning that it will be a useful tool in the fight against cancer.

- **Blueberries --** These little berries are storehouses of nutrients, and they are known for being rich in antioxidants. They will help to fight off swelling, and they can help to prevent problems like dementia and cancer.

- **Crunchy Greens** -- If it crunches and it's green, it's one of the best anti inflammatory diet foods for you to eat. Cruciferous vegetables contain more than just fiber, but they all have nutrients like antioxidants, folic acid, and vitamins to help prevent swelling.

- **Sweet Potatoes** -- These tubers are one of the best natural anti inflammatory around, as they are loaded with the nutrients that your body needs to fight the swelling. These nutrients include beta-carotene, Vitamin B6, and manganese.

- **Garlic** -- The aromatic cloves of garlic deserve their place in anti inflammatory diet recipes, as they're loaded with allicin, sulfur, and other minerals and antioxidants that are excellent at fighting swelling in your body.

- **Ginger and Turmeric** -- These two spices are loaded with nutrients, and both of them will help to prevent swelling in the body.

- **Green Tea** -- The antioxidants in the tea make this your beverage of choice for your anti inflammatory menu, and you'll find that there are many delicious ways that you can prepare this swelling-preventing tea!

What foods should you stay away from while on you anti inflammatory diet?

- Sugar, refined sugar, processed syrups, artificial sweetener. Use natural honey, molasses, and the natural sugar found in fruits to add sweetness to your food.

- Trans fats, saturated fats, cheap cooking oils, oils that have a high saturated fat content, peanut butter, margarine, most vegetable oils, and partially hydrogenated oil.

- **Alcohol.**

- Dairy products such as milk, sweetened yoghurts, full fat cheese, and cream. Some natural yoghurts are acceptable, and kefir is a good alternative.

- Meats from animals that are fed grain and corn, animals that have had fat injected, and red meat. You can eat very lean meat no more than once a week, but try and eat more poultry, fish, and legumes.

- White rice, white flour, noodles, pastries, baked

goods, and any refined grains.

- Artificial ingredients, with MSG and Aspartame being at the top of the list of foods to avoid.

- Foods that cause allergic reactions. If you are allergic to foods, the allergic reaction will include swelling, which can be fatal if the swelling occurs in your throat or lungs.

Tips for Cooking and Eating Right When on the Anti Inflammatory Diet

If you're going to try the anti inflammatory diet and follow the list of anti inflammatory foods, it's important that you know how to cook. Eating right is more than just avoiding putting the wrong foods into your meals, but it's about know how to prepare the food. Here are some things you need to know about cooking and eating the right way while on the anti-inflammatory diet:

- **Make It Easy --** If you're going to be trying this diet, there are limits to what you can eat. You should try and make it as easy on yourself as possible, and you can do so by buying a variety of foods to prepare. Make sure that your diet has as much fresh food as possible, as that is the food that will be healthiest and reduce your risk of inflammation. Cut processed and artificial foods out of your diet, and make sure that you buy only the raw, healthy ingredients. Focus on eating more fruits and vegetables, and your diet will succeed!

- **How Many Calories? --** Do you know how many

calories you need to eat in order to be healthy? The average adult male needs to consume about 2,400 calories per day, while the average female needs to consume more like 1,900. The smaller you are and the less activity you do, the fewer calories you need to eat. You shouldn't have to worry about gaining weight while on this diet if you eat right, so make it a habit to eat the right number of calories in your day. Make sure that you're getting carbs, protein, and healthy fats at each meal, and you shouldn't have to worry about inflammation!

- **Watch the Carbs --** Carbohydrates are both very important and very potentially dangerous. They are the nutrients that usually lead to inflammation, especially the simple carbs found in refined, white, sugary, and processed foods. Make sure that your diet includes no more than 200 to 300 grams of carbs per day, and try to make most of those carbs healthy complex carbs from whole grains, fruits, and veggies. Your food should all be low on the Glycemic Index, and should be as free of sugar and syrup as possible. You will be only eating foods that are whole or all-natural, but you still need to watch how many carbs you eat every day.

- **Be Careful with Fats --** Red meat contains fats, as do vegetable oils, dairy products, baked goods, and many other things that you're cutting out of your diet. However, remember that fat comes in all forms, so be careful even while on the anti inflammatory diet. Stay away from the oils that have high saturated fat content, and stick with the healthier oils like sesame, peanut, and olive oil. Make sure to eat lots of nuts, fish, and avocadoes -- all of which are loaded with healthy fats that will prevent inflammation. Remove the skin from any chicken or turkey that you eat, and find the meats that are as lean and fat-free as possible.

- **Protein is Important --** While on the anti-inflammatory diet, protein is one of the most important nutrients that you can eat. You're going to be cutting way back on carbs and fat, so you'll need to keep your body healthy by loading it with healthy proteins. Proteins like fish, tuna, and legumes are your best options, but chicken, turkey, and even lean meat can be part of your diet. You shouldn't eat more than 120 grams of protein per day, and make it lean and natural proteins as much as possible. Vegetable protein from beans and tofu are your best option to stay healthy while on this anti inflammatory diet.

- **Load the Fiber --** Seeing as you are trying to flush all of the inflammation-causing nutrients out of your body, it's in your best interest to speed up the flushing process. There are few nutrients that are as effective at getting rid of toxins and inflammation-causing chemicals as fiber, which comes from legumes, whole grains, and raw foods. Your best option is to eat as much of these foods as possible, as they will contain the nutrients that will keep your body healthy while you're trying to get rid of the unhealthy toxins and chemicals that are causing problems. You need to get at least 40 grams of fiber in your diet per day, so eat more fiber-rich foods while on the anti inflammatory diet for the best results!

- **Get Lots of Nutrients --** You need vitamins and minerals, as well as fatty acids and antioxidants. You can get these nutrients from all manner of places, though fruits and vegetables are some of the best sources. Carrots contain Vitamin A, citrus fruits contain Vitamin C, avocadoes contain Vitamin E, and berries, green tea, and red grapes contain healthy antioxidants. Make sure to get enough of the nutrients to stay healthy while on the anti inflammatory diet.

Are You Cooking Right?

If you're cooking, you may be using more oil than you realize. If you're going to try this healthy diet, it's important that you cook the right way. Here are some cooking methods to stick with while on the anti inflammatory diet:

- **Poaching --** Cooking your food in water instead of oil may seem like a bad idea, but your food will come out just as tasty if you poach it correctly. You can use chicken broth to make the food taste better, and you'll find that soup base makes a great liquid for poaching. It will help your food to be healthier, and it will be equally delicious.

- **Baking --** Baking is the best way to keep your oil consumption limited. You don't actually need oil to bake food, but a bit of fat helps to keep the food tasty. Use olive or sesame oils for baking, and make sure that your food is in the center of the baking tray in order to enable air to circulate around the food. If you marinate the food before baking it, it will be juicy and moist. You can also use tin foil to cover the baked food, as it will trap the liquid inside the food.

- **Stir-Frying --** If you're going to cook your food

with oil, you should use the stir-frying method made popular in China. The food doesn't sit in the oil - which stimulates the production of trans fats - but it will be just as tasty. The food doesn't absorb a lot of oil, and it will be much healthier.

- **Steaming** -- For vegetables, steaming is the best way to go. You won't have to do more than place the veggies in a steamer to get them to come out just right, and you can enjoy lightly-cooked veggies within minutes. Just make sure not to overcook them, as that will leech the nutrients out of the veggies.

- **Grilling/Broiling** --One of the best things about broiling and grilling your food is that it will not require any oil, but the natural juices in the food will make it tasty. Grilling is ideal if you have a grill, but a broiler is like a grill in the oven for those who don't have an easy-to-use grill. You will find far less fat in your food, and it will be a whole lot tastier!

It's very important that you avoid deep frying, frying, and microwaving your food. Boiling will leech the nutrients out of the food, unless you're making a soup that will utilize the water in which it was boiled. Make sure to cook the right way, and your food will be a whole lot healthier!

Now that you know what to eat and what not to eat - as well as how and how not to cook your food - you're ready to get started with the many recipes for your anti inflammatory diet!

Good luck, and happy eating!

Delicious Anti Inflammatory Recipes

Baked Teriyaki Chicken

This delicious dish will be perfect when served for dinner, and you'll find that it will be an absolutely delightful meal to enjoy any day of the week!

Ingredients:

For this dish, you will need:

Two chicken breasts
1 tablespoon of cornstarch
Water
Soy sauce
Orange juice
Rice or apple cider vinegar
Garlic
Fresh ginger root
Black pepper
1 cup of brown rice

Preparation:

To begin, chop two cloves of garlic into very small pieces, dicing it as finely as possible. Place a large skillet on the stove to heat, and pour a tablespoon of sesame oil into the pan. Once the sesame oil is hot, add the garlic into the bottom of the skillet, and cook for a minute - until the garlic begins to turn golden.

Drop the rice into the skillet, and cook the rice until it starts showing signs of toasting. Pour in 2 cups of water, and let it cook with the lid on. The rice will usually take about 35 minutes to cook properly, but check it occasionally to ensure that it doesn't burn.

As the rice is cooking, slice the chicken breast into four pieces. Rub the pieces of chicken breast with a little bit of salt and black pepper, and place them in a baking tray. Heat the oven to 350 F.

In a saucepan on the side, combine 3 tablespoons of orange juice with ½ cup of soy sauce and ¼ cup of vinegar. Apple cider vinegar will make the sauce a bit sweeter. Stir until the liquid is hot and nearly boiling, and drop the tablespoon of cornstarch into the pan. Stir for a minute, and turn off the heat.

Chop 4 cloves of garlic and about one tablespoon of

fresh ginger root, and use the chopped aromatics to rub down the chicken once again. Pour the sauce over the chicken, ensuring that all of the breasts are covered equally.

Place the chicken in the oven, and let it cook for at least 15 minutes. Check to ensure that the chicken is properly cooked by inserting a knife. Make sure that the chicken is properly cooked, and that there is no raw meat in the center of the breast.

Serve the chicken on a bed of brown rice, and enjoy!

Polynesian Chicken

This fascinating recipe combines savory chicken with sweet fruit, and it will be a unique dish that will make your mouth water.

Ingredients:

For this dish, you will need:

3 chicken legs and thighs
1 peach
¼ pineapple
1 bunch of grapes
Salt and pepper, to taste
Garlic
Sesame oil

Preparation:

To begin, remove the skin from the chicken. Cut the chicken in half, separating the legs from the thighs.

Turn the oven on, and let it heat to 350 F.

Dice the peach, pineapple, and grapes, and squeeze 1 orange and 1 lemon into the bowl of fruit to add some sweet flavor.

Dice the garlic very finely, and use it along with the salt and pepper to rub down the chicken. Add sesame oil to season the chicken, and place them in a baking tray. Top with the fruits, and place the chicken into the oven.

Give the chicken about 45 minutes to cook, as you will want to turn the heat down to about 325 F in order to avoid burning the fruits. Make sure the chicken is completely cooked by inserting a fork into the thickest part of the chicken, until it touches the bone. If no blood comes out, the chicken is properly cooked.

Remove the chicken from the oven, and transfer it onto a plate. Serve with barley, couscous, quinoa, or brown rice.

Turkey Tenderloins

If you just can't stand the thought of spending all day preparing Christmas dinner, this is a quick and easy meal that you can make that will be just as tasty!

Ingredients:

For this dish, you will need:

2 pounds of turkey tenderloins
Soy sauce
Dijon mustard
Rosemary
Salt and pepper, to taste
Garlic
Onions

Preparation:

To begin, place the turkey tenderloin in sealable plastic bags.

In a bowl, combine ½ cup of soy sauce with 2 tablespoons of Dijon mustard and 4 teaspoons of crushed rosemary. Add salt and pepper as desired, and mix thoroughly. Dice the onions and garlic as finely as possible, or run them through a food processor before adding them into the mixture.

Once the sauce is properly mixed, pour some of the sauce into each bag. Shake the bag well to ensure that the liquid has coated the turkey tenderloins completely, and place the bags in the fridge.

The turkey should sit in the fridge for at least 3 or 4 hours, as that will ensure that the meat has absorbed the flavor of your marinade. You may want to give the bags a shake every hour, as that will ensure that both sides are coated with the liquid.

Preheat the oven to 350 F when you are ready to cook the turkeys. Remove the turkey tenderloins from their bags, and place them in an oven tray or broiler pan - depending on your desired doneness of the turkey. Let them broil or bake for about 25 minutes, checking to ensure that the turkey is properly cooked. Poke it with a knife to check for doneness, and the turkey will be properly cooked when the juices run clear.

Slice the turkey, and serve with the rest of your dinner.

Turkey Curry

This fantastic dish will enable you to use all those leftovers from Christmas dinner, or you can use ground turkey if you want a delicious variation on a traditional Indian dish. It may be a bit spicy, but it's guaranteed to be absolutely delightful!

Ingredients:

For this dish, you will need:

Sesame oil
Ground cinnamon
1 onion
4 cloves of garlic
Fresh ginger root
Turmeric root
Water
2 green chili peppers
1 pound of turkey meat (ground or diced turkey)
Red chili powder
Garam masala
Salt and black pepper, to taste
2 cups of brown rice

Preparation:

To begin, place the rice in a skillet to cook. You will need about 2 cups of water per cup of brown rice, but add an extra half cup to ensure that the rice doesn't turn out crunchy once it's done cooking. Place a lid on the rice, and leave it to cook for about 40 minutes.

Place another skillet on the stove to heat, and add in 2 tablespoons of sesame oil into the pan. Add half a teaspoon of cinnamon into the pan, and mix it in with the oil. When the oil gets hot, the cinnamon's scent will be released.

When you can smell the cinnamon, add the diced onions into the pan. Cook them until they are golden brown, and add the garlic in to cook for about a minute. Dice 1 tablespoon of ginger root and 1 teaspoon of turmeric root, and add them into the pan to cook with the garlic. The ginger and turmeric should cook for about three minutes in order to release all of their flavors into the food.

Once the aromatics have cooked, add ¼ cup of water into the pan. Bring the water to a boil, and let it thicken the roots. Cut the two green chilies in half, and add them into the pan. Add the turkey, a teaspoon of spicy chili powder, and ½ teaspoon of garam masala. Add another half cup of water, and place a lid on the curry as it cooks.

You will want to let the curry cook for about 10 more minutes, as that will ensure that the turkey is properly cooked. Once the mixture has thickened into a sauce, add a bit of salt and pepper for flavor. Taste the sauce, and add water to thicken it if necessary.

Serve over the brown rice, and enjoy!

Noodle-Free Turkey Lasagna

This dish will be the perfect addition to your anti inflammatory diet menu. You'll be able to enjoy the classic taste of the dish, but without having to worry about noodles, red meat, and ricotta cheese causing swelling in your body. It tastes great, but it's a lot lighter than your average lasagna.

Ingredients:

For this dish, you will need:

1 pound of ground turkey
8 large tomatoes
1 onion
5 cloves of garlic
Basil
Thyme
Oregano
6 ounces of Cottage cheese
4 zucchini
Salt and pepper, to taste

Preparation:

To begin, cut the onion in half, and add half into a pot -

along with 3 cloves of garlic. Cut the tomatoes in half, and place them in the pot to stew. The tomatoes will need to cook for about an hour, as that will soften them and make it easier to run them through your food processor.

Puree the tomatoes after an hour of cooking, and place them back into the pot to continue cooking. Add in salt and black pepper, as well as a teaspoon of fresh basil, a pinch of thyme, and a teaspoon of oregano. Stir the sauce well, and let it cook for another hour. (Add water as needed as the liquid boils down).

Once the sauce has cooked properly, remove it from the stove. Dice the other half of the onion and the two remaining garlic cloves, and place them in a skillet with a tablespoon of olive oil. Cook the aromatics until they are golden brown, and add the ground turkey into the skillet to cook. Make sure that the ground turkey has been cooked properly, and remove the skillet from the stove.

Add a bit of salt, pepper, garlic, and oregano into the cottage cheese, and use the cottage cheese. Slice the zucchini into thin strips, and place them in a baking tray - as you would lay out regular lasagna noodles.

Pour tomato sauce onto the zucchini, and scoop the

ground turkey onto the first layer. Cover with a layer of zucchini, more tomato sauce, and the cottage cheese. Continue adding layers until the tray is full, and the ingredients are all used up.

Preheat the oven to 350 F, and place the trays in the oven to bake. It will take about 20 minutes for the zucchini to cook, and you can remove the trays from the oven and serve while the lasagna is still hot!

Black Bean Huevos Rancheros

This Mexican recipe is the perfect breakfast, and you'll find that the delicious addition of black beans makes it a very healthy meal that will be surprisingly filling!

Ingredients:

For this dish, you will need:

4 eggs
2 tomatoes
1 onion
1 green chili pepper
1 cup of canned black beans
¼ pound of turkey or soy bacon
Salt and pepper, to taste

Preparation:

To begin, dice the bacon into small pieces. Place a skillet on the stove to heat, and fry the bacon in the bottom of the pan. Once the bacon is becoming crispy, add the black beans into the mix. Cook the beans until the liquid is boiling and the beans are hot.

In a separate pan, add a tablespoon of olive oil, and

place the pan on the stove to heat. As the pan is heating, dice the onion very finely. Add the onion into the pan, and cook until golden brown.

While the onions are cooking, dice the tomatoes into small cubes. Add them into the pan, and let them cook for about 5 minutes. Add salt and black pepper, as desired.

Dice the chili pepper into very small pieces, and add it into the pan with the other ingredients. Let the chili cook until it is soft, and remove the ingredients from the pan. Return it to the stove, and add a tablespoon of olive oil once again as the pan heats.

Crack the eggs into a bowl, and beat the eggs thoroughly to combine the yolks and the whites. Pour the eggs into the pan, and cook them as scrambled eggs. Once they are properly cooked, add the tomato mixture and the black beans into the dish. Mix the eggs together with the other ingredients well, and serve with some brown flour tortillas and homemade salsa!

Quinoa Breakfast Cereal

Need a healthy, hot breakfast to get your day started off on the right foot? This delicious breakfast cereal is made with quinoa -- a low-glycemic grain that will not cause inflammation in your body. Add to that the high fiber of prunes, and you've got a breakfast for champions!

Ingredients:

For this dish, you will need:

Water
1 cup of quinoa
1 cup of prunes
1 cup of almond milk
Cinnamon
Nutmeg
Salt

Preparation:

To begin, place the quinoa in a saucepan to cook, along with a cup of water. Once the water is boiling, cover the quinoa and let it cook for about 5 more minutes - or until the grains are fairly soft. The total cooking time for the quinoa will be under 15 minutes, so keep a close eye on it.

Once the quinoa is cooked, pour in a cup of almond milk and keep the fire on low. Add in a pinch of salt, and half a teaspoon each of nutmeg and cinnamon. Remove the pits from the prunes, and add them into the quinoa to cook.

You will be able to eat the breakfast cereal once the prunes have softened, and enjoy the delicious way to start your day!

Hearty Bean Dinner

This is a wonderful dish to make on a budget, and you'll find that it will be a filling meal that will be surprisingly cheap. If you want to save money and still eat well, this is definitely the dish you should try!

Ingredients:

For this dish, you will need:

2 cups of dried beans
Water
1 onion
1 clove of garlic
1 stalk of celery
1 potato
3 tomatoes
½ pound of soy or turkey bacon
1 tablespoon of honey
1 bunch of cilantro
Salt
Mustard powder
Oregano
Black pepper, to taste

Preparation:

To begin, place the dried beans in a large pot to cook, and add about 4 cups of water for every cup of beans. Drop the onion, the head of garlic, the celery stalk, and the potato into the water -- leaving them whole and unpeeled.

Set the pot on the stove to cook, and let the beans boil for about 3 hours. You'll want to add a bit of salt into the beans as they cook, and let them cook until the skin of the beans will crack when you blow on them.

Once the beans have cooked properly, use a ladle to fish out the onion, garlic, potato, and celery. Throw these into the garbage, as they will have absorbed all of the gas from the beans -- but will have released their flavors into the legumes.

Dice the tomatoes into cubes, and add them into the beans. Pour 3 cups of hot water into the beans, along with a tablespoon of salt and black pepper each. Place the beans back on the stove, and let them cook.

As the beans continue cooking, place a skillet on the stove for the bacon. Cook the bacon in the pan until it is golden brown, and add it into the beans -- along with any oil that is produced by the bacon.

Add the cilantro into the pot, and use a teaspoon of mustard powder and oregano each to add flavor to the beans. Let them cook until you can smell the variety of flavors, and let the beans boil for a few minutes to ensure that they absorb all of the delicious tastes.

Serve while hot.

Quinoa and Black Beans

If you want a healthy, low fat meal to enjoy while on your anti inflammatory diet, this is definitely a dish for you to enjoy! It will have almost no effect on your blood sugar levels, as both quinoa and black beans are low GL foods. It is a delicious meal that will fill you up easily and quickly!

Ingredients:

For this dish, you will need:

Sesame oil
1 onion
5 cloves of garlic
1 cup of quinoa
Cumin
Cayenne pepper
Salt and pepper
2 ears of corn
1 can of black beans
Fresh cilantro

Preparation:

To begin, place the quinoa in a pot with water, and place

the pot on the stove to cook. You'll need about a cup of water per cup of quinoa, but add a bit extra water just to be safe. The quinoa will take about 15 minutes to cook on medium heat, so keep a close eye on it.

Place the ears of corn in a pot, and add enough water to cover the corn. Bring the pot to a boil, and cook until the corn is soft. Remove the corn from the pot, run them under cold water to cool them down, and use a knife to remove the kernels of corn from the cob. Place the corn kernels in a bowl and set them aside.

Place a skillet on the stove to heat, and add a tablespoon of olive oil into the pan. Dice the onion and garlic very finely, and add them into the stove to cook as well. Cook them until they are golden brown, and add the quinoa into the pan to cook as well. Mix the quinoa well to ensure that the flavors of the garlic and onions are absorbed into the grain.

Once the quinoa has been stirred into the aromatics well, add a teaspoon of cumin and ½ teaspoon of cayenne pepper. Add the black beans and the ears of corn, as well as half a bunch of cilantro -- chopped before adding, of course.

Mix the ingredients together well, let them cook for a

few more minutes, and serve while hot.

Meaty Beans and Rice

This dish is guaranteed to have your kids begging for more, even if beans aren't their favorite food. It's a recipe that's quick and easy to make, and you'll find that the dish will be a popular one with your whole family.

Ingredients:

For this dish, you will need:

1 pound of ground turkey or chicken
1 cup of dried beans
2 onions
1 head of garlic, plus 5 cloves
1 potato
3 tomatoes
Tabasco sauce
Brown Rice
Water
Cumin
Crushed red pepper
Oregano
Salt and pepper, to taste

Preparation:

To begin, place the beans in a pot with 4 cups of water per cup of beans. Place the pot on the stove to heat, and drop 1 whole onion, 1 head of garlic, and the whole potato into the beans. This will absorb the gas, and will add the flavor into the beans.

Let the beans cook for about four hours, or until blowing on the beans will cause the skin to crack. Once they are cooked, use a ladle to scoop out the onion, garlic, and potatoes, drain the water from the beans, and return them to the stove with three cups of water added to the pot.

Dice the tomatoes into small cubes, and add them into the pot of beans. Dice half of the other onion, as well as three cloves of garlic. Add them into the pot, and let the beans cook for about half an hour more.

As the beans are cooking, place the brown rice in a pot on the stove to cook, using about 1 cup of brown rice and 2 ½ cups of water. Bring the brown rice to a boil on high heat, and turn the fire to low heat to let the rice cook until it is soft. Add more water as needed to prevent the rice from burning.

Place a skillet on the stove to heat, along with a tablespoon of olive oil. Dice the two remaining cloves of garlic, along with the remaining half onion. Cook them until they are golden brown, and add the ground meat into the pan. Brown the meat before adding a tablespoon of crushed red pepper, a teaspoon of cumin, and a teaspoon of oregano. Add salt and pepper as desired. Finish cooking the meat, and remove from the stove.

The beans should be cooked by now, so remove them from the pot they are in and pour them into a skillet on the stove. Pour in half a cup of almond milk, as well as salt and black pepper. Use a masher to mash the beans, making sure that 90% of the beans are properly mashed.

Pour the refried beans into the pan with the meat, and mix them well before serving over a bed of brown rice.

Lentil Soup

If you are feeling chilled on a cold winter day, there's nothing like a hot bowl of soup to help you warm up! This delicious soup contains all of the nutrients you need to stay healthy, and you'll find that it will be the perfect meal to eat when the weather turns chilly.

Ingredients:

For this dish, you will need:

1 cup of lentils
Olive oil
1 onion
4 cloves of garlic
2 carrots
2 celery stalks
4 large tomatoes
Salt
Black pepper
Bay leaves
Water
Fresh parsley
Paprika

Preparation:

To begin, place the lentils in a bowl, and fill the bowl with drinking water. Leave the lentils to soak in the water overnight, as that will help them to cook a lot faster - and will eliminate the gas from the legumes.

Come the next day, drain the lentils, run water over them again to rinse them out, and drain them thoroughly.

Place a soup pot on the stove, along with a couple of tablespoons of olive oil. Dice the garlic very fine, and add it into the pot. As the garlic is cooking, dice the onions to be added once the garlic has turned slightly golden. Dice the celery stalks as well, and add them once the onions have become partially translucent. Add the carrots in next, and stir fry everything in the soup pot for a few minutes.

Before you add in the lentils, drop a teaspoon of paprika, a couple of bay leaves, a tablespoon of salt, and as much pepper as you want into the onions. Sauté everything together for a few minutes, and finally add in the lentils.

Add enough water to cover the lentils completely, working with about 4 cups of water per cup of lentils.

Bring the water and lentils to a boil. Dice the tomatoes into small cubes, and add them into the boiling soup. The water will cook the tomatoes quickly, and turn it into a delicious soup. Don't forget to add the parsley before removing the soup from the stove and serving while hot.

Chicken and Lentils

If you want a unique dish that will make your mouth water and your stomach rumble, this is the one for you. You'll find that it takes a bit of work to make, but it's absolutely fantastic and an excellent choice for any occasion!

Ingredients:

For this dish, you will need:
Olive oil
2 large chicken breasts
1 onion
3 carrots
4 cloves of garlic
1 cup of lentils
Salt
Cilantro
4 tomatoes
Rosemary
Basil
Thyme
1 lemon
Black pepper, as desired

Preparation:

To begin, place the lentils in a mixing bowl, and fill the bowl with water. Leave the lentils to soak overnight, as that will eliminate the gas and make the lentils easier to cook. The following morning, drain the lentils, rinse them well, and drain them once again before setting them aside.

Place a skillet on the stove, and add a few tablespoons of olive oil into the bottom of the pan. Slice the chicken breast from the bone, and cut each breast into three pieces. Cook the pieces in the skillet, making sure that the breast is properly cooked before removing it from the fire.

Heat the skillet once again with oil, and dice the onion to add into the pan. Cook until tender, and add the diced garlic into the pan. Dice the carrot as well, and add it into the pan to cook for about 5 minutes.

Cut the tomatoes into cubes, and bring them to a boil on the stove. Cook them until they are nice and saucy, and they will turn into a thick tomato sauce.

Once the carrots have cooked, transport the aromatics into a soup pot, heat the pot, and add the lentils into the pot. Mix them around to coat them with the flavor and the oil from the aromatics, and pour 3 cups of water into the pot. Add as much salt as you want, and let the lentils cook for about 20 minutes once the water has begun to boil.

Place the chicken back in the used skillet, and continue cooking on low heat for a few more minutes. Transport the chicken into the pot with the lentils once they're cooked, and stir well to ensure the chicken is coated with the flavor.

Add the tomato sauce into the pot, as well as a teaspoon each of basil and rosemary. Let the lentils keep cooking with these added ingredients for another 5 minutes or so, and serve with a dash of lemon juice for flavor.

Curried Lentils

Nothing makes a good curry like some lentils mixed with chicken, and you'll find that this exotic dish will be just what you need to help you fill up on a healthy meal. With the addition of brown rice or quinoa to the mix, you can make a healthy, filling dinner!

Ingredients:

For this dish, you will need:
½ cup of lentils
1 can of unsweetened coconut milk
Curry paste
Salt
Water
2 chicken breasts
Quinoa
8 cloves of garlic
1 onion

Preparation:

To begin, place the lentils in a bowl, and fill the bowl with water. Place the bowl in the sink, and let the lentils soak overnight. This will make them easier to cook the next day, and will eliminate a lot of the gas. Come morning, drain the lentils, rinse them, drain them again, and set them aside.

Place the lentils in a sauce pan, and add a cup of water into the pan. Turn the heat to high, and bring the lentils to a boil. Once they are boiling, add a tablespoon of curry paste and the coconut milk. Stir well to ensure that the ingredients are mixed, and add a pinch of salt. Cover the curry with a lid, and turn the heat on low to allow the lentils to simmer gently.

In a separate skillet, add a tablespoon of olive oil. Dice 5 cloves of garlic and ¾ of the onion, and sauté them in the bottom of the skillet.

Cut the chicken breasts into small cubes, and cook them in the skillet with the aromatics. Once the chicken is nearly cooked, add it into the curry mixture and mix well. Return the lid and let the lentils continue cooking.

Place the skillet back on the stove to heat, and add a tablespoon of olive oil. Dice the remaining garlic cloves and the rest of the onion, and sauté them in the bottom of the pan. Add 1 cup of quinoa, and cook until the quinoa shows signs of becoming toasted. Add 1 ½ cups of water, and turn the heat down to medium to allow the quinoa to cook. It will take about 15 on medium heat, so make sure to watch the quinoa.

Once the quinoa is cooked, serve it onto a plate, and scoop the curried lentils on top. Add a dash of lemon for flavor, and garnish with a sprig of parsley or cilantro.

Maple-Flavored Salmon

If you're a fish lover, salmon is the best of the best! You'll find that the rich taste makes it incomparable, and the fatty acids in the fish make it excellent for preventing inflammation. This recipe will help you to make a fish that you just can't help but love!

Ingredients:

For this dish, you will need:

1 pound of salmon fillets
¼ cup of natural maple syrup (not the artificially produced kind)
Soy sauce
4 cloves of garlic
Salt
Black pepper
Fresh ginger root
1 lemon

Preparation:

To begin, combine the maple syrup in a bowl with about half a cup of soy sauce. Add in a pinch of black pepper, half a tablespoon of salt, and the minced garlic. Add half a tablespoon of chopped fresh ginger root, and a dash of lemon. Stir well to combine all of the ingredients.

Place the salmon fillets in a baking tray with a bit of olive or sesame oil coating the bottom of the tray. Preheat the oven to 350 F.

Pour the sauce over the fish fillets, and set the tray in the fridge to marinade while the oven is heating. Once the oven is hot, place the baking trays in the oven, and let the salmon cook without a cover for about 20 minutes.

The salmon will be ready to eat once it flakes when you press on it with a fork.

Grilled Salmon

If you're a fan of grilled fish, this is a recipe that you can't help but love! You'll find that it's absolutely fantastic when you make it on a wood-fire grill, but you can cook it up on the stove or a propane grill if you want. It will be just as tasty, and a lot less work to prepare!

Ingredients:

For this dish, you will need:

1 pound of salmon
Balsamic vinegar
1 lemon
Soy sauce
Salt
½ an orange
Fresh ginger root
Paprika
Black pepper
Red pepper flakes
5 cloves of garlic
3 green onions
Sesame oil
Peanut oil

Preparation:

To begin, slice the salmon into steaks. It will be easier to marinade and rub the fish if it's already sliced up.

In a bowl, combine ¼ cup each of soy sauce and balsamic vinegar with the juice from one large lemon. Add in the juice from the orange, and dice or grind the garlic and ginger very finely to add them into the mix. Add in a teaspoon each of black and crushed red pepper, paprika, and sesame oil, and as much salt as you think it needs. Dice the green onions, and add them into the mixture. Stir well to combine.

Pour the sauce over the fish, and use your hands you rub the various ingredients into the fish gently. Add a bit of peanut oil, and transfer the salmon fillets into Ziploc plastic bags. Pour the sauce into the bags, and shake to coat the fish with the liquid completely. Set the steaks in the fridge to marinade, and let them sit for about an hour as you fire up the grill.

You want the heat of the grill to be medium high, so either turn down the propane grill or wait until your wood fire has mostly burned down to red coals. Remove the salmon fillets from their bags, place them on the grill, and cook them until they are tender and flaky. Use a brush to apply some of the liquid, and they will taste heavenly once you're done!

Baked Garlic Salmon

This is a delicious fish dish that you can't help but love, and you'll enjoy the rich flavor of this amazing salmon. Even those that aren't partial to fish will find this recipe entirely enjoyable, and it's one of the best anti inflammatory recipes that you can prepare!

Ingredients:

For this dish, you will need:
1 pound of salmon
4 cloves of garlic
Fresh dill
1 lemon
3 green onions
Salt and pepper, as desired

Preparation:

To begin, turn the oven to 425 F, and let it heat as you go about preparing the fish.

Slice the salmon into steaks, ensuring that they're neither too thick nor too thin. Spray some cooking spray on aluminum foil, and place the salmon steaks onto the foil.

Sprinkle a bit of salt and black pepper onto the fish, as your taste demands. Dice the garlic and the onions very fine, and add a bit of the aromatics into the foil with the fish. Slice the lemon, and place one or two thin slices on each piece of fish. Add the fresh dill -- chopped, of course -- as the final touch.

Once the fish has been seasoned, use a piece of tin foil to cover the top of the fish - wrapping it tightly to ensure that the juices will not leak out. Place the wrapped fish steaks in a baking tray, and place the tray in the oven.

The salmon should take about 20 to 30 minutes to cook, and you can check to see that the salmon is done by pressing on the steaks with a fork. If it flakes easily, they're ready to eat.

Salmon Ceviche

This recipe comes from South America, specifically Peru - the land of the Incas. It's a unique dish that will surprise you, and it's an absolutely fantastic one when it's made right.

Ingredients:

For this dish, you will need:

1 pound of sushi-grade salmon (it is fresh enough to eat raw)
¼ tablespoon of natural brown sugar
Salt
Chili sauce
3 Limes
Black pepper
Cumin
Olive oil
2 cloves of garlic
1 small red onion
1 tomato
Fresh cilantro
1 avocado

Preparation:

To begin, add the brown sugar into a bowl with ½ teaspoon of chili sauce and 2 tablespoons of salt. Stir well, adding the juice from the three limes into the bowl. Add ¼ teaspoon each of cumin and black pepper, along with the same amount of olive oil.

Dice the garlic and the onion very fine, and stir them into the bowl. Dice the tomatoes and the cilantro, and add them into the mix. Cut the salmon into bite-sized cubes, and stir the salmon gently into the other ingredients.

The salmon will need to sit in the fridge overnight, though you can eat it after about 4 to 6 hours. Drain the liquid from the salmon, cut the avocado into cubes, add the cubes into the mix, and serve the delicious fish dish cold with whole wheat crackers.

Mixed Veggie Salad

If you want to keep cool during the summer, this delicious salad will definitely be the ideal dish for you! It will be a refreshing veggie dish that will go well with any meal, or you can even make a hearty main dish out of it by adding fish or chicken.

Ingredients:

For this dish, you will need:
1 head of lettuce
1 tomato
1 red onion
1 ear of corn
1 cucumber
1 head of cabbage
1 bunch of spinach

Preparation:

To begin, place the spinach and lettuce in a bowl to soak. Make sure to wash the spinach well, as you want to get all of the dirt out from among the leaves.

Dice the tomato into cubes, and place them in a bowl. Slice the onion into rings, and add them into the bowl as well.

Place a stock pot on the stove to heat, and add the ear of corn into the pot with 2 cups of water. Bring the water to a boil, and cook the corn until you're sure that it's properly tender. Use a knife to cut the kernels from the ear, and add the kernels into the salad.

Slice the cabbage very finely, and do the same for the lettuce. Cut the spinach into thin strips, and add the three leafy vegetables into the salad.

Cut the cucumber in half, and scoop out the majority of the slightly bitter seeds from inside. Slice the cucumber into small pieces, and add them into the salad. Toss the salad well, and add the dressing of your choice for a refreshing mixed vegetable delight!

Grilled Chicken Cranberry Spinach Salad

If you want a hearty salad that will be very filling, this is the one for you for! You'll be able to get all of the nutrients that you need, and without eating any simple carbs or refined foods. Just from the salad, you'll be filling your body with all the healthy nutrients that will keep it running!

Ingredients:

For this dish, you will need:

1 large chicken breast
1 bunch of spinach
½ cup of cranberries
½ cup of nuts (pecans, almonds, etc.)
¼ cup of poppy seeds
½ red onion
¼ cup of white wine vinegar
¼ cup of apple cider vinegar
¼ cup of peanut or olive oil
Salt and black pepper, to taste

Preparation:

To begin, slice the chicken breast into medium sized

pieces. You should get about 12 pieces from the chicken breast.

Place a skillet on the stove, and cook the chicken with a tablespoon of olive oil in the bottom of the pan. Make sure that the chicken's juices run clear, and remove them from the pan to cool in a plate on the side.

Slice the spinach, or use your hands to rip it apart. Add the cranberries, nuts, and poppy seeds into the bowl, and toss the salad.

Dice the red onion very finely, or run it through your blender. Mix the vinegars and the oil together, and use them to dress the salad. Toss the salad gently, and top with the grilled chicken breast.

Delicious Cucumber Salad

This salad will be an absolute delight, and you'll find that it will be one of the most enjoyable salads that you can eat while on the anti inflammatory diet. It's easy to make, and it requires very few ingredients to prepare.

Ingredients:

For this dish, you will need:

2 cucumbers
3 tomatoes
1 red onion
Mayonnaise
White vinegar
Salt and black pepper, to taste
Dill

Preparation:

To begin, slice the cucumbers in half. Cut the halved cucumbers into slivers, making sure that they are thin enough to eat easily. (Note: The peel on some cucumbers will be very bitter, so peel them if necessary.) Cut the tomatoes into slivers as well, and add them into the bowl with the cucumbers. Cut the onion into thin rings, and stir them in with the cucumbers.

In a separate bowl, combine 3 tablespoons of vinegar with a tablespoon of white vinegar. Add salt and pepper as desired, and mix the dressing in with the vegetables.

Tofu Salad

If you're a tofu lover, this is definitely the salad for you! It's loaded with all the healthy nutrients your body needs, and you'll find that it will be a surprisingly filling side dish despite the fact that it's mostly made with vegetables.

Ingredients:

For this dish, you will need:
1 package of firm Tofu
Korean sweet chili sauce
Ginger root
2 cloves of garlic
Soy sauce
Sesame oil
1 cup of snow peas
2 carrots
1 head of red cabbage
1 cup of peanuts

Preparation:

To begin, combine the chili sauce with a tablespoon each of soy sauce and sesame oil in a bowl. Dice the garlic until it's very fine, and crush the ginger. Add both of the aromatics into the sauce, and stir well. Cut the tofu into cubes, and add it into the sauce. Place the mixture into the fridge, and let it marinate in the cool fridge for about an hour.

Place a pot of water on the stove to heat, and leave the pot on high heat until the water is boiling. Turn the water to medium heat, and drop the snow peas into the water. Let them sit for about 3 minutes, and scoop them out with a slotted spoon. Place them in a bowl of cold water to cool off for a few minutes, and drain them before setting them aside.

Slice the cabbage very finely, and use the grater to grate the carrots into long, thin strips. Chop the peanuts as much as you can.

Add the carrots into the bowl with the cabbage, and add the snow peas as well. Toss the vegetables to mix them, and add the dressing with the tofu to complete the flavor. Garnish the salad with peanuts, and serve.

Tofu Scramble

If scrambled eggs in the morning aren't your thing, you may find that this delicious tofu scramble will be your best option! It's a vegetarian's dream, and it's a delightfully low fat meal that you can enjoy at any time of the day!

Ingredients:

For this dish, you will need:
1 pack of firm silken tofu
Olive oil
1 onion
4 cloves of garlic
1 green bell pepper
2 potatoes
2 green tomatoes
Salt

Preparation:

To begin, peel the potatoes and cut them into bite-sized pieces. Place them in a pot on the stove, along with enough water to cover the potatoes. Turn the heat on high, and bring the potatoes to a boil. Cook them until they are just soft enough to spear them with a fork, and remove them from the heat.

In a skillet, place a tablespoon of olive oil. Dice the garlic very fine, and add it into the bottom of the skillet. Once the garlic has turned slightly golden brown, add the potatoes into the skillet. Cook them until the potatoes are properly tender, and remove them from the pan.

Place the skillet back on the stove, along with two tablespoons of olive oil. Dice the onions as the oil is heating, and add them into the skillet to cook. Once the onion has become tender and slightly transparent, add the green bell pepper -- which you will have de-seeded and diced. Cook until the bell pepper is soft.

Dice the green tomatoes, and add them into the skillet. Cook them until they begin to release their juices, and add the salt as desired. Add the potatoes into the mix, and cook for a few more minutes.

Once the potatoes are properly coated with the juices of the tomatoes, add the tofu into the pan. You will need to mash it using a masher or a fork, as that will make it much easier for you to scramble. Mix the tofu in with the rest of the ingredients, and let it cook until it gets nice and hot.

Serve with bran muffins or whole wheat toast

Baked Tofu

This is a dish that you'd never expect to enjoy, but it's surprisingly enjoyable! Even if you aren't a tofu enthusiast, it's very likely that you'll love the taste of this dish. It may take time to get used to, but it's a healthy meal that will grow on you with time.

Ingredients:

For this dish, you will need:
1 pack of firm tofu
Soy sauce
Sesame seeds
Ginger
Honey
1 cup of brown rice
Water

Preparation:

The night before you are going to eat the dish, crush the ginger and add it into a bowl with 3 tablespoons of soy sauce. Remove the tofu from the package, and drain it thoroughly before putting it into a Ziploc plastic bag. Pour the soy sauce mixture into the bag, and shake it to coat the tofu. Place it in the fridge to marinate overnight. In the morning, turn the tofu over to allow the other side to marinate properly.

Place the brown rice in a pot with 2 ½ cups of water, and cover the rice with a lid once the water has begun to boil. It will take the rice about 45 minutes to cook completely, and you may have to add a bit more water to ensure that it doesn't burn.

As the rice is cooking, toast the sesame seeds in a pan. Keep the fire on low heat, and add about ½ cup of the seeds into the pan once it is already hot. It will take about three minutes to toast the seeds.

Once the seeds have been toasted, let them cool off on a plate, and sprinkle the cool seeds onto the tofu once you have removed it from the plastic bag. Preheat the oven to about 350 F, and place the tofu into the oven to bake for about 8 minutes once it has heated properly. Make sure to pour the remaining marinade over the tofu, and serve the baked tofu on a bed of rice -- sprinkled with the rest of the seeds.

Lime and Cilantro Tofu

This is a unique Tofu-rich twist on a classic Latin American dish, and you'll find that it has all the great taste that you've come to expect from Mexican and South American food. It's a rich dish that will set your mouth watering immediately.

Ingredients:

For this dish, you will need:
1 pack of extra firm tofu
Cilantro
4 cloves of garlic
2 limes
Soy sauce
Cumin
Natural brown sugar
Cayenne pepper
Olive oil

Preparation:

To begin, dice fresh cilantro until you have about a handful of the green stuff - or ¼ cup. Dice the garlic very finely, and add it into a bowl with the cilantro. Grate the zest from the 2 limes, and add it into the bowl with the garlic. Squeeze the lemon juice, and add it into the bowl as well. Add in a teaspoon and a half of soy sauce, a teaspoon of the cumin, half a teaspoon of brown sugar, and half a teaspoon of cayenne pepper. Pour in about a tablespoon of olive oil, and mix all of the ingredients together well.

Open the package of tofu, drain the liquid, and add the large cube of extra firm tofu into a Ziploc plastic bag. Pour the marinade into the bag, and shake the tofu gently to coat it with the liquid. Once it has been properly coated, place it in the fridge to marinate. You can leave it overnight if you want, or it will be good to eat in about an hour.

Once the marinating is done, remove the tofu from the bag - using a slotted spoon to allow the liquid to drain off the tofu.

Place a skillet on the stove to heat, and add a tablespoon of olive oil into the bottom of the pan. Place the marinated tofu in the skillet, and cook it until it has been evenly browned on all sides. Apply the marinade each time you flip the tofu, and that will ensure that it absorbs all of the delicious flavor. It will take about 15 minutes to cook, and you can serve the cooked tofu on a bed of brown rice.

Tofu Watercress Salad

This delicious salad will be the perfect side dish for a hearty meal, or it will help you to stay faithful to your diet. It's a very low fat and low calorie dish, but it's loaded with the healthy nutrients that your body needs!

Ingredients:

For this dish, you will need:
Bean sprouts
1 pack of firm tofu
2 cans of tuna
2 tomatoes
1 bunch of watercress
Pickled radish
½ red onion
4 cloves of garlic
Sesame oil
Soy sauce

Preparation:

To begin, pull out a baking dish to prepare the salad in. Cover the bottom of the tray with bean sprouts, and follow it with a layer of tofu. Drain the tofu and slice it into thin pieces to lay on top of the bean sprouts. Open the cans of tuna, drain the liquid, and layer the tuna on top of the tofu.

Cut the watercress into strips, and add a layer on top of the tuna. Dice the tomatoes into small cubes, and use them to make the next layer of the salad. The top layer will be the Japanese pickled radish, and you can use as much of that as you like.

Dice the onion very fine, and place it in a bowl. Place a skillet on the stove to heat, and add a tablespoon of sesame oil into the bottom. Dice the garlic, and add it into the skillet to cook. Make sure the garlic has browned properly, and use a spoon to scoop the garlic pieces from the skillet. Add the onions into the skillet to cook, and cook them until they too are browned.

Add the garlic pieces into the salad on top of the radish, and cover the salad with the sesame oil and the cooked onions. Add half a cup of soy sauce into the salad, and stir it well to mix everything together. Serve with crackers, or as a standalone dish.

Fruit Salad

This delicious fruit salad will get your body going in the morning, or it will be the perfect dessert to enjoy after a hearty meal. The best thing about it is that it's 100% natural and healthy, so you can have it anytime and anywhere!

Ingredients:

For this dish, you will need:
Strawberries
1 red apple
1 green apple
Berries (blueberries, raspberries, etc.)
2 kiwi fruits
½ pineapple
Grapes

Preparation:

To begin, cut the stalk from the top of the strawberries. Cut the strawberries in half, and add them into a bowl.

Cut the red apple in half, and use your knife to remove the core. Cut the halves into thirds, and cut each of the resulting slices into bite-sized pieces. Repeat the same process with the green apple.

Place the berries into a colander, and run cold water over them. Raspberries can be damaged if the pressure of the water from the sink is too high, so make sure the water is gentle.

Cut the core out of the pineapple, and cut the rest into slices. Each round slice can be cut into eight pieces, and add the pieces into the bowl with the strawberries, apples, and berries.

Peel the kiwi fruit with a paring knife, and cut the ends off of the fruit. Cut the kiwi into slices, and cut each slice into quarters before adding them into the bowl.

Run the grapes under cold water, and drain them thoroughly. Cut them in half, and add the halves of the grapes into the bowl with the rest of the fruits.

Garnish with a bit of wheat germ, a sprinkling of natural brown sugar, and enjoy!

Healthy Oatmeal

If you want to start the day out with a meal that will be very enjoyable as well as filling, this is the breakfast for you. It's quick and easy to make, and you'll have no problem eating it while on the anti inflammatory diet!

Ingredients:

For this dish, you will need:

1 cup of steel cut oats
3 cups of water
1 cup of almond milk
½ cup of assorted nuts
½ cup of raisins and cranberries
Flaked coconut
Cinnamon
Vanilla
Honey

Preparation:

To begin, place a pot on the stove, and add the three cups of water into the pot. Add a pinch of salt, and bring the water to a rolling boil. Once the water has begun to boil, drop the oats into the water. Cook them for about

20 minutes, or until soft. (The steel cut oats will get soft very quickly, so keep an eye on them.)
Once the oats have cooked properly, remove them from the fire. Add the milk into the oats, and stir in the cranberries and raisins.

Use a knife to chop the nuts, and add them into the oats as well. Add a tablespoon of the flaked coconuts, and stir 2 teaspoons of vanilla extract into the oatmeal. Add two tablespoons of honey to make the oatmeal sweet, and add a pinch or two of cinnamon.

Return the pot with the oatmeal to the fire, and turn the fire on low. You will need to stir the oatmeal continuously, mixing the oats with the milk and the other ingredients. Don't let the oatmeal burn, but just leave it on the stove long enough to heat up the **oatmeal** once the oats have been added.

Serve with a sprinkling of wheat germ, sesame seeds, and amaranth seeds to make your oatmeal healthy and filling!

Banana Nut Breakfast Cereal

This is a meal that is guaranteed to keep you healthy, and you'll find that it's one of the tastiest breakfasts that you can eat. It will be loaded with nutrients, and you will definitely enjoy it once you get used to its unique, varied flavor.

Ingredients:

For this dish, you will need:

Water
1 cup of almond milk
Quinoa
1 banana
Oats
Oat bran
Cinnamon
Salt, for flavor
Assorted nuts
Brown sugar
Vanilla extract

Preparation:

To begin, place a sauce pan on the stove to heat. Add a

tablespoon of quinoa into the pan, along with ½ a cup of almond milk and a few tablespoons of water. Once the mixture has begun to boil, turn the heat down to its lowest setting.

Let the oatmeal mixture simmer for about 5 minutes, and test frequently to ensure that the quinoa is getting soft. Once the quinoa is soft, add the banana into the pan. Use a fork to mash it, and stir it in with the quinoa.

As the banana is cooking with the quinoa, add a tablespoon each of oats and oat bran. The mixture should get thicker very quickly, and it's the sign that the ingredients are cooking properly. You will need to keep it cooking on very low heat for about 5 more minutes, though stir it gently to ensure that it doesn't burn.

Once the mixture has thickened, add a tablespoon of brown sugar, a teaspoon of vanilla extract, and a pinch of salt and cinnamon each. Chop the walnuts into small pieces, and add them into the cereal to give it the delicious nutty flavor that makes it the perfect breakfast!

All of these recipes can be found online, though some of them are our own original creations. You can probably find similar recipes on websites like AllRecpes.com,

About.com, and particularly ElanasPantry.com. They are all recipes that someone made, and we just wanted to share them with you. We've made a few adjustments to the various recipes so that you'll get only our unique grain-free flavor on the recipes, but you'll find that there are many like them. The important thing is that you can enjoy your grain-free cooking and eating, and we wanted to provide you with a recipe book that you can use to prepare delicious meals free of grain and gluten. We apologize if you've seen these recipes elsewhere, and we hope that you enjoy the creations we have presented to you!

Section 2: DASH Diet

The DASH Diet is an important strategy for anyone who wants to lower their blood pressure and improve their overall health without dealing with risky medications and their side effects. This simple diet focuses on low fat, low cholesterol foods and natural ingredients, making it inexpensive and easy to follow. Plus, you'll be surprised by how delicious heart healthy foods can be. If you've been warned about the possible dangers of high blood pressure and a normal North American diet, it's time to make some changes.

The recipes contained in this book don't encompass the entire range of DASH diet options, but they will give you an idea of how you can change your favorite foods to fit the diet plan. In general, they focus on reducing the fat, cholesterol and refined carbohydrates in a dish without losing out on flavor. If you've experienced too many flavorless health foods, these recipes could be the solution that you've been hoping for.

What Is the DASH Diet?

DASH is a term that stands for "Dietary Approaches to Stop Hypertension." It is designed to be a lifestyle change for people who want to treat or prevent hypertension, also known as high blood pressure. The diet is based on studies originally performed by the US National Institutes of Health that examined three different dietary plans and their effects on blood pressure. The result is a plan that focuses on increased consumption of plant foods such as nuts, beans, low fat dairy products, vegetables and fruit.

This diet plan is recommended by the National Heart, Lung and Blood Institute for anyone who wants to decrease their blood pressure and improve heart health. In studies performed on the diet, people who followed it showed a systolic blood pressure reduction of 6mm Hg, as well as a diastolic blood pressure reduction of 3 mm Hg in patients who had tested in the high-normal range, also called pre-hypertension. In patients who had existing hypertension, the diet caused reductions of 11 mm Hg and 6 mm Hg respectively, with no change in body weight. While it was not designed for weight loss, the DASH diet's focus on lower calorie, healthier foods does make it a viable choice for people who want to reduce their body fat levels.

What Is Hypertension and Why Is It Dangerous?

Hypertension, or high blood pressure, refers to the force your blood puts on the walls of your arteries. Doctors measure it in millimeters of mercury, or mm Hg, and record it as two different numbers. They measure both the systolic blood pressure, or the pressure when your heart is beating, and the diastolic blood pressure, or the pressure between beats. A person's blood pressure can rise and fall over the course of a given day, but continued high levels can be very dangerous to your health.

When your blood flows with a lot of force, it can damage the veins and arteries, as well as organs like the eyes, heart, kidneys and brain. Most people who develop high blood pressure have difficulty lowering it. Left uncontrolled, this condition can lead to blindness, kidney and heart disease, and even stroke. About one in three people have high blood pressure, but many aren't aware of the problem.

Many doctors and patients turn to medication at the

first sign of high blood pressure, but this technique might not be the right one for you. Many blood pressure treatments have dehydrating effects. Others can induce depression or extreme tiredness. The very low blood pressure that is caused by some drugs can also result in severe dizziness and a tingling feeling in your fingers and toes. In more serious cases, these drugs can cause insomnia, pain in the feet, weakness and leg cramps, or an irregular heartbeat. That's a lot of risk to take when you could address the problem through less intrusive methods like diet and exercise.

How Does the DASH Diet Work?

The DASH diet provides an alternative to conventional, drug-based methods of controlling blood pressure. It is designed to help you maintain a healthy weight with moderate levels of physical activity. It focuses on reducing sodium levels, which have been shown to elevate blood pressure in some people. It also includes decreased levels of saturated fat and cholesterol, which contribute to narrowing of the arteries and can make it hard for blood to cycle properly.

Over time, this diet can help patients who have high blood pressure lower their levels and reduce their medication requirements. In some cases, it can even allow you to discontinue use of medication entirely. It is important to change your dosages only on the recommendation of a doctor, however. Don't stop using your high blood pressure medicine just because you've started using the DASH diet.

DASH Study Daily Nutrient Goals

The studies used to formulate the DASH diet set a few standard daily nutrient goals, which are also used in the main plan. Following this diet means trying to keep your total fat intake to about 27 percent of your daily calories. Saturated fat should make up only about 6 percent of your calories, however. The DASH diet is relatively high in carbohydrates, which should make up about 55 percent of your daily calorie intake, but most of the carbohydrates you eat should be complex ones, rather than those derived from white flour and sugar.

The DASH diet also recommends trying to keep your daily cholesterol intake below 150 milligrams. The original studies aimed for a sodium intake of 2,300 milligrams or less, but more recent research suggests that 1,500 milligrams or less is even better for reducing blood pressure. It's a good idea to get at least 30 g of fiber and 1,250 milligrams of calcium each day while on this diet, as well.

DASH Diet Guidelines

All those number can be hard to understand, so the researchers who wrote the DASH diet plan broke it down into clearer recommendations. They suggest eating six to eight servings of whole grain per day, four to five servings of vegetables, and four to five servings of fruit. Consuming two to three servings of low fat dairy products provides protein and calcium. If you eat meat, aim to consume six or fewer one-ounce servings of lean meat, poultry or fish per day. Vegetarians can substitute an egg for one serving of meat.

The DASH diet guidelines recommend consuming four to five servings of nuts, legumes and seeds per week, though vegetarians should increase these to replace meat. Fats and oils should be kept to a relative minimum of two to three servings per day. This includes, mayonnaise, margarine and salad dressings. Sweets need to be eaten in moderation; the DASH diet recommends having five low-fat servings or fewer every week. Very active people can increase servings of grain, fruits and vegetables, low fat dairy and lean meat to help support their higher metabolisms.

Using DASH for Weight Loss

The DASH diet wasn't originally designed to help people lose weight, but it can be adapted to help you maintain a healthier weight and reduce your risk of high blood pressure. Doctors recommend simply using the lower calorie recommendations for the diet to cut back your energy intake. Eat a little less than you normally would and focus on getting about 30 to 60 minutes of regular physical activity, like walking or swimming, every day. Your weight may not decrease dramatically, but it should drop slowly over a longer period of time. Experts recommend this kind of loss because it is the most likely to be permanent.

Intuitive Eating with the DASH Diet

While many people like to start out counting their calories to ensure they're getting the right level of nutrition on the DASH diet, this doesn't work for everyone. If you have trouble with calorie counting, or if you've been on the diet long enough to know your choices are good ones, it might be time to look at intuitive eating. This technique involves paying attention to the signals your body is sending. When you've mastered intuitive eating, you'll provide food when your body is hungry, stop eating when it sends signals of fullness, and avoid snacking for emotional reasons or out of boredom. This method can be very helpful for people who tend to have trouble with more mathematical techniques, but it does take some practice.

Intuitive eating is compatible with the DASH diet from the beginning, but you'll need to modify your strategy a little bit. Start out by focusing on the low calorie foods that are acceptable on this diet. That means consuming more fruit and raw, non-starchy vegetables while eating more calorically-dense foods in small amounts. Even if you have a craving for nuts, beef or cheese, try having just a few bites to begin with. You may be able to conquer your craving quickly without overeating.

Making DASH Dieting Easy

The transition period between a normal North American diet and the DASH technique can be a rocky one, especially if you don't know how to find tasty snacks or eat at your favorite restaurants. Make things simpler by keeping pre-cut fresh fruit, vegetables and low-calorie dairy snacks in your refrigerator at all times. That way, when you want to grab something simple, they'll be right at your fingertips.

Make eating out on the DASH diet easier by turning the menu into a treasure hunt. You may be surprised by how many healthy foods you can find. Most restaurants now offer a veggie burger instead of a beef burger. You may also be able to choose steamed vegetables or fresh fruit rather than French fries or onion rings. Choose a garden salad with a light oil and vinegar dressing in restaurants that don't offer many vegetable options, and be sure to take part of your meal home. You'll find eating out on the DASH diet much simpler than you expected.

Last, but not least, practice sneaking DASH foods into your ordinary meals. It's easy to add cucumber slices, shredded cabbage or carrots to an ordinary sandwich. If you usually consume tea or coffee, add a full glass of skim milk to it to boost protein without increasing your cholesterol. Vegetable broths and fruit purees provide a great way to ensure you're getting all your fruits and veggies: just drink them!

Exercise and the DASH Diet

The DASH diet works well on its own, but when paired with exercise, it has considerably better effects. In one study of 124 men and women over the age of 50, 30 minutes of aerobic exercise three times per week lower blood pressure and weight much more quickly than diet alone. If you need to make lifestyle changes in order to improve your blood pressure and reduce your BMI, adding light to moderate physical activity is the best way to do it.

The process is very simple. Just add a half hour of swimming, walking or other activity to your day at least three times per week. The workout doesn't need to be severe. In fact, you should be able to hold a conversation while you're getting your exercise. Try to recruit a workout buddy to help keep you on track and develop healthy habits. You'll soon be feeling lighter and more energetic. You'll even develop more stamina, making it easier to stay active.

Recipes for the DASH Diet

These recipes are adapted from books and online sources. They range from very simple to multi-step preparations for fancier occasions, but you don't have to be a master chef to prepare them. While several of them rely on slightly unusual ingredients, you should be able to find these at many standard grocery stores. Consider checking the ethnic or natural foods section for low-sodium soy sauce, chili paste and other less common ingredients. The extra flavor they give to your meals makes it worthwhile to seek these foods out.

You don't have to jump straight into preparing just DASH diet recipes, either. You can incorporate a few of these dishes into your normal routine, increasing them until you're eating healthy all week long. That's what makes the DASH diet such a good idea. It helps you make healthy decisions and incorporate them into your life without having to turn your normal way of eating upside down. If you care about the health of your heart, arteries and brain, it may be time to try out some of these great DASH recipes. In just a little while, you won't know how you ever lived without them.

Appetizers

DASH Spinach Dip

This cheesy dip eliminates the cholesterol-laden cream cheese and full-fat sour cream normally used in spinach dips, substituting velvety Great Northern beans and low fat dairy. Instead of heavily-salted ingredients, it relies on flavorful herbs and garlic to add interest. The result is a creamy dip that doesn't taste like health food. It makes a great choice for parties and goes well with sliced vegetables or warm, crusty bread.

Ingredients

2 pounds fresh spinach or 3 packages frozen spinach
1 pound or one can cooked Great Northern beans
½ cup low fat sour cream
2 tablespoons Parmesan cheese
2 tablespoons fresh parsley
1 tablespoon fresh basil
2 teaspoons black pepper
2 cloves fresh garlic

Wash and drain the fresh spinach or thaw and drain if you are using frozen products. Drain the beans and mash or puree until smooth. Combine all ingredients and stir until well combined, then pour into an oven-safe dish. Bake at 350 degrees Fahrenheit for about 30 minutes or until the mixture is hot throughout and bubbly.

Stuffed Portabella Mushrooms

Stuffed mushrooms are a classic appetizer, but they too-frequently contain cholesterol-packed bacon, cream cheese, eggs and other health-hazard ingredients. This version uses fresh spinach combined with garlic, tarragon and strongly-flavored cheese to provide excitement without the fat. The make-ahead element of these stuffed mushrooms means they're the perfect last-minute choice when you have company or just don't want to spend too much time in the kitchen

Ingredients

4 large portabella mushrooms
1 cup fresh or frozen spinach
4 teaspoons grated Parmesan cheese
1 tablespoon fresh tarragon
2 teaspoons olive oil
2 cloves fresh garlic
½ teaspoon black pepper

Crush the garlic and remove the stems from the portabella mushrooms. Chop the stems finely. Drain the spinach thoroughly. Heat 1 teaspoon of olive oil over medium-high heat in a heavy pan and sauté the garlic, pepper and tarragon for one minute. Add the mushroom stems and spinach leaves to the pan, sautéing 3 to 4 minutes or until stems are tender. Remove and place in a bowl. Add remaining 1 teaspoon of olive oil to the pan and place the mushrooms in the pan, cap-side down. Saute for 3 minutes without stirring or turning.

Flip the caps, cover, and reduce heat to low for another 2 minutes. Remove and place the caps on a foil-lined baking sheet with the gills facing up. Fill each mushroom with ¼ of the spinach mixture. Top with Parmesan cheese. If you are making the recipe ahead, cover the sheet with plastic wrap and place it in the refrigerator or freezer until ready to serve. Otherwise, place the mushrooms on a rack 6 inches below your broiler and cook for 3 to 4 minutes, until the cheese has just browned.

Crispy Coconut Chicken Fingers

Coconut shrimp is a perennial favorite, but it's also loaded with saturated fat and cholesterol. This healthier alternative uses chicken thighs to offer just as much flavor in a better-for-you package. Combined with the sweet and spicy dipping sauce, this recipe will be a hit at your next party. Vegetarians and vegans can also enjoy this dish; just substitute tempeh for the chicken and egg replacement powder for the egg white as preferred.

Ingredients

½ pound boneless, skinless chicken thighs
¼ cup no-sodium bread crumbs
¼ cup unsweetened coconut flakes
1 teaspoon powdered garlic
1 egg white
¼ teaspoon black pepper
Dipping Sauce
2 tablespoons orange marmalade
1 ½ teaspoons rice vinegar or lemon juice
¼ teaspoon cayenne pepper

Wash the chicken and pat it dry. Slice into 20 individual bite-sized pieces. Combine the bread crumbs, coconut, garlic and black pepper in a small bowl. Beat egg white thoroughly. Dip each piece of chicken into the egg, then roll in the bread crumb mixture. Place on a lightly-oiled baking sheet and bake at 425 degrees for 10 minutes. Flip each piece, then return the sheet to the oven for another 10 minutes.

Combine all sauce ingredients in a small bowl and stir to combine. Arrange the chicken bites on a platter around the bowl of sauce and serve right away.

Vegetable Sushi

When you mention sushi, most people assume raw fish or eggs will be involved, but the term "sushi" actually refers to the slightly sour rice. You can top this delicate Japanese food with all kinds of ingredients, including fresh and colorful vegetables. Use brown rice to add more fiber and a nutty flavor. You can mix and match the vegetables in this recipe, making it an excellent choice to use up leftovers.

Ingredients

1 cup short grain brown rice
1 1/2 cups water
1 tablespoon plain rice vinegar
1 package sushi nori seaweed sheets
Vegetables
steamed or roasted asparagus spears
avocado
roasted beets
fresh cucumber strips
pickled daikon or radish
shredded kale
roasted sweet potatoes
roasted kale
fresh or sautéed mushrooms

thin slices of tomato

Place the brown rice in a pan or rice cooker brown and rinse until the water runs clear. Drain and add 1 ½ cups of water. Cook until the rice is tender. Sprinkle with vinegar and add salt substitute to taste. Stir with a wide, flat spoon or a rice paddle and allow the mixture to cool.

To assemble, place one sheet of nori on a bamboo sushi mat. Spoon approximately ½ cup of the cooked rice mixture in a thin layer across the whole piece of nori. Place shredded kale, asparagus stalks, cucumber strips or other vegetables on top of the rice, then roll the seaweed over the vegetables and into a long log, using the mat to keep it intact. Place the finished roll seam-side-down on a cutting board and slice into pieces with a very sharp knife. Serve immediately with pickled ginger, low sodium soy sauce, horseradish or sesame seeds.

Fresh Mushroom Quesadillas

Mushroom quesadillas are a popular dish in Mexico, where they are referred to as quesadillas de hongo. Unlike processed American versions of Hispanic cuisine, this dish is light and healthy without being dull or flavorless. Say goodbye to fatty, uniform Mexican fast food and hello to healthy flavor with these spicy but savory tortillas.

Ingredients

1 pound fresh mushrooms
1 medium onion
1 cup shredded Swiss cheese
¼ cup low fat sour cream
3 cloves garlic
2 tablespoons fresh cilantro
1 fresh jalapeno pepper
1 teaspoon olive oil
1 package low sodium, whole grain flour or corn tortillas

Finely chop mushrooms, onion, jalapeno, cilantro and garlic. Heat 1 teaspoon of olive oil in a heavy pan over medium heat and sauté the alliums and mushrooms for about 10 minutes, or until tender and lightly browned. Season with black pepper to taste. Heat a large skillet to medium-low and place a single tortilla on the surface, flipping to warm throughout. Sprinkle with cheese, chopped jalapeno and cilantro. Allow the cheese to melt, then spoon on a small amount of the mushroom mixture. Add a second tortilla and flip the entire quesadilla over. Remove to a plate to cool and repeat until you have used all the cheese and mushroom mixture. Slice each quesadilla into quarters or eighths, depending on the size of your tortilla. Serve warm with low fat sour cream.

Beverages

Peanut Butter and Banana Smoothie

Whether you'd like to enjoy a smoothie for breakfast, dessert or a between-meal treat, this one is a great choice. The banana provides plenty of natural sweetness, while the peanut butter offers monounsaturated "healthy" fats and protein. Combined with non-fat milk, this could be the perfect pick me up when you're feeling tired. Vegans can substitute unsweetened soy or almond milk.

Ingredients

1 cup skim milk
1 medium banana
1 tablespoon creamy natural peanut butter, unsalted

Peel and slice the banana. Place in a blender or food processor and add the milk and peanut butter. Process until completely smooth. For a more milkshake-like version, freeze the banana before blending.

No-Booze Margarita

Most people on the DASH diet need to take alcohol in moderation, while some need to eschew it completely. This tasty beverage offers the same overall flavor as a margarita, but without the alcohol. That means you can drink it at any time!

Ingredients

2 cups ice
½ cup lime juice
2 tablespoons simple syrup
Sliced limes for garnish
Simple Syrup (makes 6 tablespoons):
¼ cup raw sugar
¼ cup water

Combine the water and sugar in a small saucepan over medium heat, stirring until the sugar has dissolved completely. Remove to a sealed container and refrigerate for up to a week.

Combine syrup, ice and lime juice in a blender or powerful food processor. Process until a smooth slush has formed. Pour into a chilled glass and garnish with lime slices.

Sugar-free Agua Fresca

Aguas fresca, sweet non-carbonated beverages popular in Mexico and the southeastern US, can be a refreshing choice for hot days. Unfortunately, most of these drinks contain large quantities of white refined sugar. This variation uses fresh fruit to provide the sweetness, making it a much healthier and lower-calorie option you can enjoy more often.

Ingredients

3 pounds watermelon
½ cup unsweetened cranberry juice
½ cup apple juice
¼ cup lime juice
1 lime

Remove the seeds and rind from the watermelon, cutting it into fine dice. Place it in a food processor or blender and process until a smooth puree is produced. Sieve this puree to remove the excess pulp, yielding a clear, delicious juice. Cut the lime into thin slices. In a large pitcher, combine the watermelon juice, cranberry juice, apple juice and lime juice. Stir to combine completely. The mixture may be slightly cloudy, but it will taste delicious when refrigerated and garnished with a slice of fresh lime.

Spicy, Sweet and Tangy Herbal Tea

Technically a tisane, because no tea leaves are involved in its brewing, this drink can be served either warm or chilled. It uses only natural, unprocessed sweeteners, making it an excellent alternative to sodas and conventional iced tea beverages.

Ingredients

1 ½ quarts water
½ cup fresh mint
1/3 cup lemon juice
3/8 cup strongly-flavored honey
4 tablespoons fresh ginger
1 medium lemon

Peel and chop the ginger. Slice the lemon thinly into rounds. Combine the ginger, water and lemon juice in a saucepan and bring to a boil over high heat. Reduce to low and allow to simmer for 5 minutes. Add the mint, remove from heat entirely, and allow to steep for 5 to 8 minutes. Use a fine sieve to remove the mint leaves and ginger, which can be discarded after use. Stir in the honey and serve warm or cold with a lemon slice floating on top.

Non-Alcoholic Hurricane Punch

Traditionally made with rum, this beverage is a great choice to add lots of vitamin C and other antioxidants to your diet. When made with ice, it becomes a delicious frosty drink that's perfect for a hot summer day.

Ingredients

2 cups or 1 can fresh unsweetened pineapple
1 orange
1 lemon
1 lime
½ cup unsweetened cranberry juice
1 cup ice (optional)

Peel the citrus fruit and set aside. Chop the pineapple roughly into chunks and combine in a blender with the cranberry juice and citrus. Add the ice if you are using it and process until the mixture is a smooth liquid or frosty puree. Serve in tall glasses with a spoon for the icy version.

Breakfast

Chewy Fruit Bars

This simple bar is sweet and hearty, making it the perfect choice for breakfast on the go. Unlike many ordinary granola bars, it's not high in fats or refined sugars, however. Natural ingredients such as multigrain cereal and bran help keep the glycemic index low, while walnuts, dried fruit and almond butter provide the energy your body needs to keep going. Enjoy these bars as a quick snack or even a light dessert in a pinch.

2 cups dry whole grain hot cereal
1 cup bran flakes cereal
¾ cup honey
¾ cup low salt almond butter
½ cup non-fat dry milk
½ cup dried apricot pieces
½ cup dried cranberries
½ cup walnut pieces
1 tablespoon canola or light olive oil
1 tablespoon vanilla extract

In a large bowl, combine cereals, nuts, dried fruit and dry milk. Place almond butter, honey and oil in a small saucepan and heat to medium-low, stirring constantly. Allow mixture to bubble, then remove the pan from the heat and add vanilla extract. Pour this mixture over the fruit and cereal, stirring until completely combined. Grease a baking pan with canola oil or line it with parchment paper. Spread the mixture into the pan, patting it down tightly. Bake for 20 minutes at 325 degrees and set aside to cool on a rack for 20 minutes or until firm. Cut into 12 pieces and store in an air-tight container at room temperature.

Broiled Almond-Banana Toast

Bananas are a classic breakfast ingredient, but on their own they tend to be carbohydrate-heavy and unsatisfying. That's why this morning treat pairs fresh banana with fiber-rich whole grain toast and protein-packed almond butter. Putting the finished product under the broiler caramelizes the natural sugars in the banana, producing a delicious, gooey result that you'll also enjoy as a snack.

Ingredients

2 slices whole grain bread
2 tablespoons smooth almond butter
1 small banana
ground cinnamon and nutmeg to taste

Toast the bread and arrange it on an oven-safe plate or a small baking sheet. Spread each slice with 1 tablespoon of almond butter. Slice the banana into rounds of medium thickness and arrange them on top of the almond butter. Sprinkle the surface with cinnamon and nutmeg, then place under the broiler for 2 to 3 minutes, or until the almond butter melts slightly and the bananas begin to brown. Allow to cool and eat with your fingers, or dig in right away with a fork.

DASH-friendly Oatmeal

Oatmeal naturally has properties that make it good for your heart, but many commercial instant products contain large amounts of sugar, sodium and other unhealthy ingredients. If you love a hot, hearty bowl of oats in the morning, this low-cholesterol, salt-free option will satisfy you without cutting back on taste. Fresh fruit and nuts add to the oatmeal's flavor and nutrition profile, making this a breakfast recipe you're sure to love. Try it out on a cold winter morning.

Ingredients

1 ½ cups unsweetened almond milk
1 cup old fashioned rolled oats
¾ cup mixed berries or other chopped fruit
1/8 cup whole pecans
¼ teaspoon vanilla extract
Cinnamon to taste

Combine the almond milk and vanilla in a small sauce pan over medium-high heat. Bring to a gentle simmer and add the oats. Cook, stirring occasionally, for about 5 minutes or until almost all the liquid has been absorbed. Stir in the fruit and serve topped with pecans and cinnamon.

Healthy Homemade Granola

Traditional granolas are full of healthy ingredients such as whole grains, nuts and fruit, but they tend to be heavy on the fat, salt and added sugar. The situation gets worse in the case of some packaged granolas, which add preservatives and other artificial ingredients. This homemade granola recipe is nutritionally dense and concentrates on healthy fats and natural, relatively unrefined sources of sugar. Flax seeds add an extra omega-3 punch, making this recipe a great way to start your day.

Ingredients

3 cups old-fashioned rolled oats
1 cup sliced almonds
1 cup raisins or dried cranberries
4 tablespoons flax seed
¼ cup raw sugar
1/4 cup honey
¼ cup sunflower or canola oil
½ teaspoon vanilla extract
½ teaspoon ground sugar
½ teaspoon allspice
½ teaspoon ground ginger

Combine the oats, almonds, flax, spices and sugar in a large bowl, mixing thoroughly. In a separate bowl combine the honey, oil and vanilla extract. Pour the wet ingredient mixture into the dry ingredients, mixing with a spatula as you pour. Stir until the dry mixture is wet throughout. Lightly grease one to two cookie sheets with sunflower oil or another monounsaturated fat. Pour the wet granola into the pans, patting it into place if necessary. Bake in a 250 degree Fahrenheit oven for 90 minutes or until dry and lightly browned, stirring every 15 minutes. Break up chunks of granola as you stir to create the appropriate consistency. Allow the mixture to cool, then combine with the dried fruit and store in an air-tight container.

Toasted Breakfast Sandwich

Not every DASH-friendly breakfast recipe is sweet. There are also plenty of savory options that combine fresh vegetables with low-sodium, low-cholesterol proteins for a heartier start to your day. If you love eggs for breakfast, this recipe will help you enjoy them without the heart risk associated with large amounts of egg yolk. Flavorful mustard and tomatoes keep the open-faced sandwich interesting, so you won't miss the fat.

Ingredients

2 egg whites
½ cup fresh spinach leaves
1 slice whole grain bread
1 small tomato
1 ½ teaspoons olive oil
1 teaspoon prepared brown mustard
½ ounce slice reduced-fat cheddar cheese
Black pepper and paprika to taste

In a small pan, heat the olive oil to medium-high. Beat the egg whites and add to the hot oil, scrambling them until completely solid. Add the spinach and heat until wilted. Spread the mustard onto the bread and place it on an oven-safe plate or baking sheet. Arrange tomato slices on top of the mustard, then top with the egg mixture and thinly-sliced cheddar cheese. Sprinkle with black pepper and sharp paprika to taste. Bake in an oven or toaster oven at 400 degrees Fahrenheit until the bread is crisp and the cheese is melted and slightly browned.

Main Dishes

Simple Grilled Chicken

This basic chicken dish is easy to make on any outdoor grill. It combines the low cholesterol and white meat of bone-in chicken breasts with flavorful garlic and spices. The finished product is crisp, golden brown and caramelized for an intense flavor. You won't miss the extra fat!

Ingredients

4 bone-in chicken breasts with skin
2 cloves garlic
salt-free herb seasoning mix

Heat a gas or charcoal grill to medium heat. Fold non-stick aluminum foil into a boat shape for each chicken breast. Cut the garlic cloves in half and rub the cut surfaces over the skin of the chicken breasts. Sprinkle with seasoning mix to taste and place the chicken breasts in the boats, skin side down. Grill for 45 minutes or until the center reaches 160 degrees Fahrenheit, turning the chicken once every 10 to 15 minutes.

Basic Barbeque "Pork" Chops

Barbecued pork may sound unhealthy and decadent, but you can substitute other meats to make your favorite pork recipes compatible with the DASH diet. This recipe uses "chops" of boneless chicken thighs, since the dark meat provides similar flavor intensity to that of lean pork. Just make sure you don't overcook it, as the meat can easily dry out with too much heat. Add a fresh salad and this dish is ready to make a complete meal!

1 ½ pounds boneless chicken thighs
10 ounces low sodium condensed tomato soup
3 tablespoons red wine vinegar
2 tablespoons low sodium Worcestershire sauce
1 small onion
¾ cup water
1 teaspoon sharp paprika
1 teaspoon chili powder
¼ teaspoon cinnamon
¼ teaspoon black pepper
1/8 teaspoon cloves

Trim all fat from the chicken, cube, and set aside. Combine all other ingredients in a large bowl, then transfer to a large skillet with high sides. Heat to medium and add the chicken cubes, simmering for 30 minutes or until cooked thoroughly. Serve with bread or 2/3 cup of brown rice.

Miso-Marinated Cod

This spicy Asian fish recipe provides plenty of healthy polyunsaturated omega-3 fatty acids, along with the rich flavors of miso and chili paste. If cod is unavailable, use any firm, flaky white fish that can be cut into thick steaks. Avoid thin species like flounder, which will not cook correctly. While the marinade itself is very salty, the practice of wrapping the fish in a porous material prevents too much salt from getting into the food itself. To make this dish ahead, simply apply the marinade, then freeze the entire dish. Defrost slowly in the refrigerator before cooking normally.

Ingredients

1 pound cod
3 tablespoons low-salt sweet white miso
1 tablespoon garlic-chili paste
2 tablespoons apple juice
2 tablespoons unprocessed cane sugar, such as turbinado

Mix together all raw ingredients except for the fish. Take a piece of plastic wrap and spread it over the counter or a cutting board, then apply a layer of miso marinade a little larger than the total surface area of the fish. Place a piece of cheesecloth on top of the marinade layer. Wrap the cheesecloth around the fish, then apply marinade to the top side. Wrap the plastic around the fish and its wrapping, then place the plastic bundle into a freezer bag. Place in the refrigerator for two hours to overnight.

Remove the fish from the refrigerator and peel away the plastic and cheesecloth layers. Heat a large nonstick frying pan over medium heat and place the fish in it. Cook on both sides until the fish is opaque and flaky throughout. Serve with low-sodium miso soup, rice and Japanese pickles. Discard any unused marinade for safety reasons.

Blackened Beef

Thinly sliced lean top round beef seared with strong spices makes for an exciting and flavorful main dish, especially when you pair it with stewed potatoes, onions and carrots. Finish the dish with tender greens for a recipe that's tasty and nutritious. This blackened beef dish is especially good with crusty low-sodium bread.

Ingredients

1 pound lean top round of beef
6 medium red potatoes
4 large onions
3 large carrots
2 cups low-sodium beef broth
2 cups water
2 cloves garlic
1 bunch kale
2 tablespoons sharp paprika
1 tablespoon dried oregano
1 teaspoon chili powder
1 teaspoon powdered garlic
½ teaspoon black pepper
¼ teaspoon red pepper
¼ teaspoon mustard powder

Place the beef in the freezer until partially frozen. Cut the potatoes into quarters, mince the garlic cloves, slice the carrots into rounds and remove the stems from the kale. Chop the onions very finely to yield about 4 cups. Combine paprika, oregano, garlic powder, chili powder, red and black peppers and dry mustard in a small bowl with a lid. Set aside. Remove beef from freezer and slice it across the grain in strips about 1/8 inch thick. Sprinkle with the seasoning mix, covering all available surfaces. Lightly grease a large heavy skillet or stockpot then preheat over high. Add the meat strips and sear, stirring continuously, for about 5 minutes.

Add the broth and water to the pan to deglaze, then add potatoes and garlic to the skillet. Allow the blackened spices to float to the top. Cover and lower heat to medium, cooking for about 20 minutes or until potatoes are tender. Add the carrots and place the kale on top of the dish. Cover and cook for an additional 10 minutes. This dish can be served right from the skillet or pot.

Feta-ricotta Greek Pizza

Many DASH dieters find that they miss conventional pizza after they start their new healthier way of eating. Getting onto the DASH diet doesn't mean you can't enjoy this classic treat, however. This whole-grain, Greek-inspired recipe provides richness with reduced fat ricotta and feta cheese, plus plenty of tasty vegetables. Adding fennel, mint and olive oil gives this recipe an authentic Mediterranean flavor. Once you learn to make these pizzas at home, you won't miss delivery.

Ingredients

10 ounces fresh or frozen spinach
3 ¼ cups low sodium marinara sauce
1 ¼ cups reduced-fat ricotta cheese
1 ¼ cups fresh mint
1 cup fresh fennel
1 whole grain 14 inch pizza crust or equivalent dough
¾ cup feta cheese crumbles
4 plum tomatoes
1 teaspoon strongly-flavored olive oil
1 teaspoon cornmeal
salt substitute and black pepper to taste

Heat a pizza stone or cookie sheet in the oven at 500

degrees Fahrenheit. Sprinkle a pizza peel with cornmeal to prevent sticking. If you are using a pizza crust, follow package instructions to prepare it for topping.

Chop the mint, tomatoes, fennel and spinach. Heat the olive oil in a large skillet to medium-high. Add the chopped fennel and sauté for five minutes, or until slightly translucent. Reduce the heat to medium-low. Drain all water from the spinach and add it to the fennel. Season with black pepper and salt substitute according to your preferences. Place the raw dough on the pizza peel and transfer it to the baking stone or sheet. Cook for 5 minutes at 500 degrees and remove from oven.

Spread the sauce over the pizza crust, then top with the spinach and fennel mixture. Spoon the ricotta in small quantities over the vegetable mixture, but do not try to spread it. Add feta crumbles and bake for another 15 minutes, or until the crust is cooked completely and the edges are lightly browned. Combine the mint and tomatoes in a separate bowl, then sprinkle them over the surface of the pizza before cutting.

Chinese Restaurant Ginger Beef

American-style Chinese food is rarely compatible with the DASH diet, but many people still miss its exciting flavors. The good news is that you can make your own at home, using far less grease, corn syrup and artificial flavors. You'll retain all the best things about restaurant Chinese dishes and avoid the sometimes sticky sauces and high glycemic index. This dish uses thinly-sliced lean beef, heart-friendly oils and fresh ginger to recreate a classic Chinese restaurant favorite.

Ingredients

¾ pound thinly-sliced flank or sirloin steak
1 medium onion
1 pound mushrooms
1 pound broccoli
2 tablespoons peanut oil
1 tablespoon rice vinegar
1 tablespoon fresh ginger
3 cloves fresh garlic
red pepper flakes to taste
salt substitute to taste

In a deep skillet or wok, heat 1 tablespoon of peanut oil on high. Mince the ginger and onion and add to the hot pan, frying for about a minute. Season with salt substitute to taste. Crush the garlic, slice the mushrooms and chop the broccoli. Add 1 teaspoon of garlic and the mushrooms to the pan. Cook for about 2 minutes, stirring throughout, or until the mushrooms soften and the onions become translucent. Add the broccoli and cook for about 3 minutes or until it is bright green and still slightly crisp. Remove the vegetables to a bowl.

Add the remaining tablespoon of peanut oil to the pan and allow it to heat. Add the beef strips and the remaining garlic, cooking for about 2 minutes. Sprinkle in the vinegar and red pepper flakes, followed by the vegetables. Stir to combine and remove from the heat immediately. Serve over short grain brown rice.

Vegetable Medley Pasta Sauce

The DASH diet works best when you reduce the amount of meat in your diet, but many people don't know where to start. This vegetable-based pasta sauce proves that you don't need to have sausage or beef to make a meal special. It uses readily-available dried herbs and fresh vegetables to provide great flavor without the meat. Serve it with your favorite whole grain pasta.

8 ounces canned low-sodium tomato sauce
6 ounces canned low-sodium tomato paste
2 medium zucchini
2 medium fresh tomatoes
2 small onions
3 cloves garlic
2 tablespoons olive oil
1 tablespoon dried oregano
1 tablespoon dried basil
1 teaspoon dried rosemary
1 cup water

Heat the olive oil in a medium-sized skillet. Mince the garlic and onions. Chop the zucchini and tomatoes coarsely. Add all vegetables to the pan and sauté for about 5 minutes over medium-high heat, or until the onions become slightly translucent. Mix the tomato paste and water in a medium bowl until smooth. Add to the pan, along with the tomato sauce and herbs. Cover and reduce the heat to low. Simmer for 45 minutes or until the sauce reaches the desired consistency. Season with salt substitute if desired.

Portabella Mushroom "Burgers"

Not every sandwich you eat on a bun has to be a hamburger. These grilled or pan-seared Portobello mushrooms are marinated in a tasty mixture of vinegar, garlic, cayenne and olive oil, leaving them anything but bland. When you accompany them with the traditional burger toppings, they make the perfect addition to any picnic, potluck or outdoor grilling occasion. Unlike a conventional hamburger, these sandwiches are low in calories, contain almost no fat, and are cholesterol-free.

Ingredients

4 large portabella mushrooms
5 tablespoons balsamic vinegar
2 tablespoons strongly-flavored olive oil
1 tablespoon raw sugar
1 clove garlic
¼ teaspoon sharp paprika

Wash the mushrooms and remove their stems. Place the mushroom caps in an oven-safe glass dish, stem side up. Mince the garlic and combine it with the olive oil, paprika, sugar and vinegar in a separate small bowl. Drizzle this mixture over the mushrooms. Cover and place in the refrigerator for ½ hour. Flip the mushrooms and marinate for an additional ½ hour.

Preheat the broiler or an outdoor grill to moderate heat. If cooking on a grill, lightly coat the rack with cooking spray. Grill or broil the mushrooms on a rack about 6 inches away from the flame, turning periodically and basting with marinade. Transfer to a plate and allow to rest for a few minutes before serving on whole grain buns with lettuce, tomato, onion and low-sodium pickles.

Sides

Baked Macaroni and Cheese

Macaroni and cheese are classic, hearty and comforting, but traditional recipes rely on butter, cream and very large amounts of full fat cheese. The result may be delightful to the taste buds, but it's hard on your arteries. Consider this version instead, which adds ripe tomatoes and reduced fat dairy to produce a baked dish that's delicious without harming your heart. Eat it as a side to an ordinary dinner or with a salad as a light meal all by itself.

Ingredients

2 cups whole grain macaroni
2 cups skim milk
8 ounces reduced fat cheddar cheese
2 fresh tomatoes
2 tablespoons margarine
1 tablespoon flour
1 small onion
1 teaspoon parsley
¼ teaspoon mustard powder
¼ teaspoon black pepper

Grate the cheese and slice the tomatoes and onion very thinly. Boil the macaroni in water according to package instructions, until al dente. Preheat the oven to 400 degrees Fahrenheit and melt margarine over medium-high heat in a sauce pan. Add mustard, flour, pepper and onion, sautéing until the onion becomes translucent. Stir in the milk slowly and cook until smooth and thickened. Add the cheese and stir until just melted. Drain the macaroni and transfer it to a 2 quart baking dish. Pour the cheese mixture over the macaroni and toss gently. Arrange the tomato slices on top of the dish and sprinkle with parsley. Bake for 20 minutes or until the top browns slightly.

Spicy Steamed Eggplant with Peanut Sauce

While most eggplant dishes are best served warm, this unusual side is an excellent cold option for summer. Preparation is quick and easy, and the finished recipe plates up attractively. Make this Asian-inspired dish on hot summer evenings when you don't feel like cooking. Look for long, thin purple Chinese eggplants and serve with cold noodles or rice.

Ingredients

1 ½ pounds eggplant, preferably Asian varieties
2 tablespoons crunchy peanut butter
1 ½ tablespoons low-sodium soy sauce
1 tablespoon apple juice
½ teaspoon chili paste
1 bunch parsley for garnish

Peel the eggplants using a small knife or vegetable peeler, removing the stem from each one. Wrap each eggplant loosely in damp cheesecloth or paper towels and arrange them in a circle around a microwave-safe plate or vegetable steamer. To prepare in the microwave, cook on the high setting for 5 minutes, turning once halfway through cooking. To prepare on the stovetop, steam in a large pot until the eggplant is soft and slightly translucent. Remove the hot eggplants from the microwave or pan and drop them immediately into a bowl of cold water. Remove the cheesecloth or paper towels and cut the vegetables on the diagonal into slices. Arrange on a plate with parsley and chill in the refrigerator.

For the sauce, combine all other ingredients in a small saucepan. Cook, stirring continuously, over medium-low heat until the peanut butter melts and all ingredients are well combined. Spoon over the chilled eggplant and serve.

Braised Spring Vegetables

This hearty combination of winter and new spring vegetables is a great choice when the weather is just beginning to warm. Serve it alongside your favorite meat as a side dish, or eat it on its own as a light lunch or a snack. This recipe is delicious both hot and cold!

Ingredients

1 pound small red, yellow or purple potatoes
1 large carrot
1 medium onion
1 cup green peas, fresh or frozen
½ pound green beans, fresh or frozen
1 clove garlic
½ tablespoon low-sodium soy sauce
1 teaspoon olive oil

Wash all the vegetables and cut the potatoes, carrot and onion into bite size pieces. Top, tail and snap the green beans if you are using fresh vegetables. Mince the garlic. Heat the olive oil in the bottom of a heavy skillet or pan over medium-low heat. Add the potatoes and cook for about 10 minutes or until they begin to brown, stirring occasionally. Add the carrots and cook for another 10 minutes, until both vegetables have begun to tenderize.

Add the sliced onions and garlic. Cook until they become transparent. Fill the pan with water to cover the potatoes and add the green vegetables. Cook until the beans and peas are bright green and tender, but not mushy. Season with soy sauce at the very end of the cooking process.

Rice Pilaf with Saffron

This rice dish is inspired by South Asian pilau, which often include fruit and nuts. Any brown rice will provide the nutty flavor and fiber that are ideal in this recipe, but the best choice is a very dark brown, strong-tasting rice that will provide an appealing contrast for the apricots. Serve this dish hot, as a side for curries or kebabs. If saffron is not available, you can substitute safflower or turmeric for a slightly different flavor.

2 ¼ cups vegetable stock
1 ¼ cups long grain brown rice
¼ cup pistachios
¼ cup dried apricots
3 tablespoons orange juice
1 ½ tablespoons canola, coconut or sunflower oil
¼ teaspoon saffron
salt substitute to taste

Combine the rice, stock and saffron in a medium saucepan. Bring to a boil over high heat. Reduce the heat to low and cover, simmering until the rice has become tender and absorbed all the liquid. Transfer to a large bowl. Combine the orange juice, oil and salt substitute in a small bowl. Pour this mixture over the rice. Chop the apricots. Heat a small skillet to medium and add the fruit and nuts, stirring continuously until the pistachios brown slightly and develop an oily appearance. Toss the fruit and nuts with the flavored rice to mix. Serve right away.

Spicy Garlic Green Beans

Green beans are a classic side dish for all kinds of cuisines, but too many people boil out the nutrients or serve them with copious amounts of butter. Instead of weighing down your beans, celebrate their crisp flavor with this spicy but appealing recipe. Blanching helps set the color and ensures an attractive dish, while a quick sauté with strongly-flavored
ingredients keeps the beans from blending into the background.

Ingredients

1 pound fresh, raw green beans
1 sweet red bell pepper
2 cloves garlic
2 teaspoons extra virgin olive oil
1 teaspoon dark sesame oil
½ teaspoon salt substitute
½ teaspoon chili paste
¼ teaspoon black pepper

Top and tail the beans, removing any strings, and snap them into 2 inch pieces. Bring a large pan of water to a boil over high heat and add the snapped beans. Cook for about 3 minutes, until they become bright green and crisp-tender. Remove the beans from the water and plunge them immediately into a bowl of ice water. Drain and place in a large bowl.

Remove the stem, ribs and seeds from the red bell pepper and cut it into thin strips about 2 inches in length. Heat the olive oil in a large frying pan over medium heat. Add the pepper, stir-frying for about a minute. Add the beans and cook for and additional minute. Crush the garlic and combine with the chili paste, salts substitute and pepper in a small bowl. Add this mixture to the vegetables, stirring to coat. Serve drizzled with sesame oil.

Salads

Spicy Tuna Salad

While the DASH diet emphasizes healthy foods that are lower in fat and cholesterol, that doesn't mean you can't enjoy your favorites. This tuna salad recipe relies on flavorful tomatoes, onions, limes and jalapenos, allowing you to reduce the sodium and cholesterol in other ingredients without losing out on taste.

Ingredients

12 oz. low sodium tuna (about 2 cans)
1/8 cup olive oil or low-fat mayonnaise
1 jalapeno pepper
1 tomato
1 small sweet onion
1 small lime

Drain the water from the tuna and place it in a medium bowl with the mayonnaise. Remove the stem, seeds and ribs from the pepper, dicing it finely. Dice the tomato and the onion. Add the vegetables and lime juice to the bowl and mix thoroughly. Serve with DASH-friendly crackers or bread.

Tabbouleh with Tomatoes

Tabbouleh is a mint-flavored cold salad popular in northern Africa and Western Asia. When made with whole grains, it provides plenty of nutritious fiber, along with refreshing vegetables. The tart flavor of this salad can take a little time to get used to, but it's an extremely welcome change when hot weather comes along. Serve tabbouleh on its own or as a side with kebabs or barbecued meats and vegetables.

Ingredients

½ pound whole grain bulgur wheat
½ pound cucumbers
½ pound fresh tomatoes
3 medium red onions
2 cups flat leaf parsley
½ cup fresh mint
3 lemons
1 tablespoon olive oil
½ teaspoon black pepper

Place the wheat in a large bowl and cover it with water. Soak for one hour or longer, until the grain has absorbed water and plumped. Chop all the vegetables into small cubes or dice and set aside. Drain the bulgur and mix it with the vegetables. Juice the lemons, removing the seeds but reserving the pulp. Add the lemon juice, herbs, oil and pepper to the mixture. Place it in a covered bowl and refrigerate for one to 12 hours. This salad can be stored as is for several days or up to a week with the onions omitted.

Edamame Salad

Fresh, steamed soybeans are known as Edamame in Japan, and are eaten as an appetizer or part of other dishes. When served cold, these beans also make a great salad ingredient. This recipe combines them with cherry tomatoes, fresh mint, dill and scallions. A light oil and vinegar dressing finishes it for a fresh-tasting start to any meal. Try it with a little feta or other salty cheese for added contrast.

Ingredients

½ pound fresh Edamame
1 pint cherry or grape tomatoes
¼ cup red wine vinegar
1 ½ tablespoons extra virgin olive oil
1 scallion
1 small bunch fresh dill weed
1 small bunch fresh mint
¼ teaspoon black pepper

Place the soybeans in a steamer over about an inch of water. Cover and steam for approximately 5 minutes, or until the pods are bright green and the beans are crisp-tender. Rinse with cold water and remove from the pods. Set the beans aside in a medium bowl and refrigerate. Chop the mint and dill finely. Slice the green onion. Cut large cherry tomatoes into halves, leaving small ones whole. Combine tomatoes, green onion, mint and dill in a medium bowl. Mix oil, vinegar and black pepper in a small bowl and pour over the salad. Serve chilled.

Raw Okra Salad

Many people associate okra with slimy boiled preparations or greasy fried food. This unusual member of the mallow family doesn't have to be cooked, however. When sliced carefully and served raw, it has an exciting crispness and lacks any unappealing mucilage. Combine it with spicy mixed salad greens, jicama and sweet peppers for a refreshing salad that's a little outside the usual fare.

Ingredients

1 cup fresh okra
1/3 pound fresh salad greens
1 pound jicama
1 small sweet red bell pepper
4 tablespoons low sodium poppy-seed salad dressing
¼ teaspoon salt substitute
1/4 teaspoon black pepper

Remove the stems from the okra and slice them in half vertically, using a clean, absolutely dry knife. Wipe the knife off between pieces to reduce mucilage production. Remove the stem, seeds and ribs from the pepper and cut it into strips. Peel and slice the jicama into matchsticks. Combine the okra, salad greens, pepper and jicama in a large bowl. Toss gently and season with salt substitute and fresh pepper. Top with poppy-seed dressing and serve immediately.

Tomato-Zucchini Salad with Eggs

Squash and tomatoes are abundant and at their best in the heat of summer, which is the best time to make this refreshing salad. The addition of eggs provides a little more heartiness and allows this dish to act as a light lunch or a starter. For a slightly different flavor, consider using different types of fresh herbs.

Ingredients

2 pounds zucchini
2 pounds ripe tomatoes
6 to 8 eggs
½ cup fresh basil
Dressing:
2 tablespoons extra virgin olive oil
¼ cup red wine vinegar
1 tablespoon fresh parsley
1 teaspoon raw sugar

Combine all dressing ingredients in a glass bowl and mix thoroughly. Set aside. Slice the zucchini and tomatoes into thin rounds. Bring one large and one small pot of water to a boil. Place the eggs in one pot, immediately cover, and reduce heat. Plunge the zucchini rounds into the larger pot for 2 to 3 minutes. Remove from the pot and place immediately in ice water. Drain completely and arrange alternately with the tomato slices on a large plate. Drain the eggs and place them in a bowl of ice water. Peel and slice, arranging the slices on top of the zucchini and tomato rounds. Cover with basil leaves, then drizzle vinegar mixture over the entire platter.

Low Cholesterol Potato Salad

Traditional potato salad is a must at many picnics, but it's loaded with cholesterol, fat and sodium. All of these ingredients can be hazardous for your heart, so many DASH dieters feel as though potato salad is off the menu. This recipe offers much of the same creamy taste and texture, but without the fat and salt. Bring it to your next picnic and no one will ever worry about it being "health food."

Ingredients

1 pound yellow or red waxy potatoes
1 large yellow sweet onion
2 stalks celery
1 large carrot
¼ cup reduced-calorie mayonnaise
2 tablespoons dill weed
2 tablespoons red wine vinegar
1 tablespoon prepared brown mustard

Boil the potatoes in their skins, allow to cool, and dice. Mince the onion and dill weed. Dice the carrot and celery into small pieces. Combine the mayonnaise, mustard, vinegar, pepper and dill in a large bowl. Stir in the vegetables, mixing to coat the pieces completely.

Cover and refrigerate for one hour to overnight to allow the flavors to mingle. Serve chilled.

Soups

Nutrient-packed Kale Soup

The unique, slightly-nutty taste of kale makes this soup an interesting and satisfying starter for any cold season meal, while providing a wide range of healthy vitamins. Adding homemade croutons gives this creamy recipe a hearty crunch without too much fat or too many processed carbohydrates. Plus, their freshness will help them outshine any store-bought option. Enjoy this soup whenever the weather turns chilly and kale is readily available.

Ingredients

6 cups fresh kale leaves
4 cups low sodium broth or stock, preferably vegetable
3 medium red potatoes
1 small white onion
1 tablespoon olive oil
1 tablespoon fresh thyme
1 clove fresh garlic
½ teaspoon black pepper
¼ teaspoon salt substitute
Croutons:

2 cups day old whole grain bread pieces
2 tablespoons olive oil
1 tablespoon fresh thyme
1 tablespoon fresh parsley
1 teaspoon garlic powder

Trim the kale leaves and remove any tough ribs. Chop the onion and the potatoes into small dice. Crush the garlic. Heat 1 tablespoon of olive oil in a heavy pan over medium heat and sauté the chopped onion, crushed garlic and fresh thyme for 7 to 8 minutes or until the onions are transparent. Add the diced potatoes, salt substitute and pepper. Stir well and cook for another 10 minutes or until the potatoes have begun to soften. Remove the cover and add the kale. Cook uncovered for 5 minutes, then add broth, cover and heat for an additional 5 minutes or until the kale becomes bright green and tender. Place half of the soup in a food processor or blender and process until completely smooth. Return this mixture to the saucepan and mix thoroughly.

Croutons: Cut or break bread into pieces approximately ½ inch across. Combine garlic powder, 2 tablespoons olive oil and herbs in a large bowl and add the bread. Toss to coat the outside of the bread but do not allow the oil to soak in. Place croutons on a baking sheet lined with foil and bake at 350 degrees for about 10 minutes or until the outsides are crisp and golden. Cool and use to top bowls of hot soup.

Meatless Lentil Chili

This tasty vegetarian alternative to conventional chili is hearty and flavorful, with bulgur wheat and lentils replacing the usual fatty beef and chili beans. If you're trying to reduce the number of days on which you eat meat, this chili is a great way to start. Serve with diced scallions, low fat sour cream or a DASH-friendly cornbread. For a more interesting chili, substitute red, yellow or black lentils for the traditional brown variety.

Ingredients

3 cups low-sodium vegetable broth
2 cups or one can chopped tomatoes
1 cup bulgur wheat
1 cup dried lentils
1 medium white onion
4 cloves garlic
2 tablespoons canola oil
2 ½ tablespoons chili powder
1 tablespoon cumin powder
½ teaspoon cinnamon
Salt substitute and pepper to taste

Heat the oil to medium-high in a large pot. Mince the onion and garlic, then add them to the pot and cook for

5 minutes, stirring continuously. When the alliums have become slightly translucent, add the wheat and lentils, followed by the broth. Stir to combine, then add the tomatoes and spices. Bring to a boil over high heat, then reduce to low and cover. Simmer for 30 minutes or until the lentils just begin to fall apart. Add salt substitute and pepper to taste and serve hot.

Tangy Carrot Curry

This smooth soup contains plenty of exciting spices, along with protein-rich low fat yogurt and bright, tangy cilantro. The result is an antioxidant-filled dish you'll enjoy with a fresh salad and a slice of homestyle whole-grain bread. For a spicier version, substitute cayenne or Thai peppers for the jalapeno.

Ingredients

5 cups low-sodium vegetable stock
1 pound carrots
1 large yellow onion
1 jalapeno pepper
¼ cup cilantro leaves
¼ cup low fat unsweetened yogurt
2 tablespoons lime or lemon juice
1 tablespoon sunflower oil
1 tablespoon fresh ginger
2 cloves garlic
2 teaspoons Madras curry powder
1 teaspoon black mustard seeds
salt substitute to taste

Heat the olive oil in a large saucepan to medium. Mince the garlic and ginger and chop the onion finely. Add the mustard seed to the oil and allow it to pop, then add the ginger, garlic and onion. Cook for about 5 minutes, stirring continuously, or until the onions become translucent but not brown. Remove the stem, seeds and ribs of the jalapeno and chop it finely, then add to the pan along with the curry powder. Chop the carrots roughly and sauté with the other ingredients for about 3 minutes, or until the seasonings begin to toast. Pour in about half of the stock and bring the whole pot to a boil over high heat. Reduce to medium-low and simmer for about 5 minutes, or until the carrots become tender.

Remove the soup from the pot and place it in a blender or food processor. Process until the liquid is smooth, in batches if necessary, and return to the pan. Stir in the remaining stock and reheat. Add yogurt, cilantro and lime juice, as well as salt substitute to taste. Garnish with additional cilantro and limes before serving.

Cream of Wild Rice Soup with Fennel

Traditional cream of rice soups are extremely comforting, but they're also heavy on butter, cream and refined carbohydrates, making them unsuitable for the DASH diet. Instead, consider this version. It gets its creaminess from white beans and low fat milk and includes vitamin-packed kale and carrots. If wild rice is unavailable in your area, consider substituting any long grain brown rice, such as Basmati, or red rice.

2 cups 1 percent or skim milk
2 cups low-sodium vegetable stock
1 ½ cups kale
1 cup cooked white beans, unsalted
¼ cup wild rice
2 stalks celery
1 large sweet onion
1 large carrot
1 tablespoon fresh parsley
½ tablespoon vegetable oil
1 teaspoon fennel
1 teaspoon black pepper
salt substitute to taste

Place wild rice in a small pot and cover with water. Bring to a boil over high heat, then reduce heat and simmer until the rice has become tender but chewy, or about one hour. Dice the carrot, celery, onion and parsley. Heat the vegetable oil in a large pot over medium heat, then add the onion, carrot, celery and spices. Cook, stirring periodically, until the onions are translucent, the carrots have become slightly tender. Add the parsley, kale and stock. Season with salt substitute to taste.

Combine the milk with the cooked white beans in a blender or food processor. Puree until smooth and add gradually to the soup, stirring continuously. Bring to a simmer and add the cooked rice. Simmer for an additional 30 minutes or until flavors have diffused. Serve with crusty low-sodium bread.

Hearty Turkey Soup

This recipe isn't just a way to use up the leftovers from a big holiday meal, it's also a hearty low-sodium option that includes plenty of healthy winter vegetables. Serve big bowls of this dish with rice or bread as meals on their own, or as a side for lunch or dinner.

Ingredients

Carcass from one turkey
2 quarts low-sodium chicken or vegetable broth
1 quart water
4 large yellow onions
1 large turnip
1 pound carrots
2 cups tomatoes, fresh or canned
2 cups cooked white beans, home-cooked or canned
½ pound light turkey
¼ cup hulled whole barley
1/3 cup fresh parsley
½ teaspoon black pepper
¼ teaspoon thyme
1 bay leaf
salt substitute to taste

Place the turkey carcass in a large stockpot with the

broth and water. Bring to a boil over high heat. Chop one onion into quarters and add to the pot. Reduce the heat, cover, and allow the pot to simmer for an hour. Remove all solids from the pot and place the stock in the refrigerator for 2 hours to overnight. Skim off any fat from the cooled broth and discard. Return the broth to its original pot.

Chop the carrots, turnip, tomatoes and remaining onions and add them to the broth. Add the bay leaf, beans, barley, herbs and spices to the mixture, stirring to combine. Cut the turkey meat into bite-sized chunks and add to the pot. Bring the entire mixture to a simmer, then cover and allow to cook for an hour or until all the vegetables have softened. Serve immediately.

DASH Diet 5-Day Sample Menu

Deciding how to eat on the DASH diet plan can be tricky if you're not used to dealing with its rules. Here's a quick 5-day sample menu using some recipes from this book to help you get started. There's no reason to stick to just this menu, however. You can mix and match the recipes or use foods of your own. Just make sure that you stick to the guidelines set forth earlier in this book and it'll be hard to go wrong!

Day 1

Breakfast: Fresh orange juice, whole grain toast with low-sugar fruit spread, DASH-Friendly Oatmeal

Lunch: Tangy Carrot Curry, fresh vegetable crudités, brown rice
Snack: almonds, hazelnuts or cashews, fresh peach or nectarine

Dinner: Blackened Beef, Tabbouleh with Tomatoes, Chewy Fruit Bars

Day 2

Breakfast: Healthy Homemade Granola, fresh strawberries, skim milk

Lunch: Miso-Marinated Cod, Edamame Salad, hot green tea

Snack: fat-free, low-sugar yogurt, graham crackers

Dinner: Chinese Restaurant Ginger Beef, brown rice, fresh oranges

Day 3

Breakfast: Toasted Breakfast Sandwich, fresh orange juice

Lunch: Spicy Tuna Salad on whole grain bread with lettuce and tomato,
Sugar Free Agua Fresca

Snack: Pretzels, raisins, sunflower seeds

Dinner: Feta-ricotta Greek Pizza, lettuce hearts, olives

Day 4

Breakfast: Peanut Butter and Banana Smoothie, whole

grain bagel with light cream cheese

Lunch: Meatless lentil chili, low-sodium cornbread, tomatoes, low-fat sour cream

Snack: Vegetable Sushi

Dinner: Simple Grilled Chicken, Braised Spring Vegetables, vanilla wafers

Day 5

Breakfast: Chewy Fruit Bars, Spicy, Sweet and Tangy Herbal Tea

Lunch: Tomato-Zucchini Salad with Eggs, whole grain pasta with
Vegetable Medley Pasta Sauce

Snack: apple, whole grain crackers

Dinner: Portabella Mushroom "Burgers", Low Cholesterol Potato Salad, low fat frozen yogurt

Modifying the 5-Day Meal Plan

Because every person has different calorie requirements, it's hard to say how much you'll need to eat of these foods at any given meal. If you take a little time to look at your activity level and personal habits, you'll have an easier time choosing the right calorie level for you. The main DASH diet offers 1,200, 1,600, 2,000 and 2,400 calorie options for various amounts of activity and various metabolisms. In general, if you're hoping to lose weight, consider choosing a calorie goal that's one rung lower than the one you need to maintain.

That means that if you're relatively active but overweight, you could move down from the 2,000 calories that you probably need to stay at your current weight, choosing a 1,600 calorie per day diet, instead. You'd aim to get the same 4 to 5 servings of fruits and vegetables per day, as well as the same 3 to 4 servings of low fat dairy, nuts and beans, but you'd limit your meat consumption to just 5 ounces per day and cut back on fats and sweets. It may take a little while to figure things out, but you can help it along by doubling up on low calorie vegetables, fruits and non-fat dairy while limiting meat, cheese and grain consumption.

Conclusion

The average American diet is high in unhealthy fried food and high-fat meat and dairy sources, as well as too much sugar. The result, for many people, is skyrocketing blood pressure and an increased risk of heart disease and stroke. If you're worried that your health could be at risk, it's time to take steps.

That means moving to the DASH diet and avoiding unhealthy foods in favor of rich, flavorful options that are low in fat and high in vitamins. While it's true that the adjustment period may take a little longer than you expect, all these recipes will help you make the transition. You won't miss the fat or extra sugar! Just focus on the healthy foods that you can eat and work to make fruits and vegetables a regular part of your routine. Your heart and your waistline will thank you.

www.ingramcontent.com/pod-product-compliance
Lightning Source LLC
LaVergne TN
LVHW021716060526
838200LV00050B/2691